Effective Leadership in the Family Business

A FAMILY BUSINESS PUBLICATION

Family Business Publications are the combined efforts of the Family Business Consulting Group and Palgrave Macmillan. These books provide useful information on a broad range of topics that concern the family business enterprise, including succession planning, communication, strategy and growth, family leadership, and more. The books are written by experts with combined experiences of over a century in the field of family enterprise and who have consulted with thousands of enterprising families the world over, giving the reader practical, effective, and time-tested insights to everyone involved in a family business.

, founded in 1994, is the leading business consultancy exclusively devoted to helping family enterprises prosper across generations.

FAMILY BUSINESS LEADERSHIP SERIES

This series of books comprises concise guides and thoughtful compendiums to the most pressing issues that anyone involved in a family firm may face. Each volume covers a different topic area and provides the answers to some of the most common and challenging questions.

Titles include:

All of the books were written by members of the Family Business Consulting Group and are based on both our experiences with thousands of client families as well as our empirical research at leading research universities the world over.

Effective Leadership in the Family Business

Craig E. Aronoff
and Otis W. Baskin

palgrave
macmillan

First published by the Family Business Consulting Group
Publications, 2005.

This edition first published in 2011 by
PALGRAVE MACMILLAN®
in the United States—a division of St. Martin's Press LLC,
175 Fifth Avenue, New York, NY 10010.

Where this book is distributed in the UK, Europe and the rest of the world,
this is by Palgrave Macmillan, a division of Macmillan Publishers Limited,
registered in England, company number 785998, of Houndmills,
Basingstoke, Hampshire RG21 6XS.

Palgrave Macmillan is the global academic imprint of the above companies
and has companies and representatives throughout the world.

Palgrave® and Macmillan® are registered trademarks in the United States,
the United Kingdom, Europe and other countries.

ISBN: 978-0-230-11117-2

Library of Congress Cataloging-in-Publication Data

Aronoff, Craig E.
    Effective leadership in the family business / Craig E. Aronoff and Otis
W. Baskin.
        p. cm.—(Family business leadership series)
    Includes bibliographical references and index.
    ISBN 978–0–230–11117–2
    1. Family-owned business enterprises—Management. 2. Leadership.
    I. Baskin, Otis W. II. Title.

HD62.25.A755 2011
658.4'092—dc22   2010035805

A catalogue record of the book is available from the British Library.

Design by Newgen Imaging Systems (P) Ltd., Chennai, India.

First Palgrave Macmillan edition: January 2011

10 9 8 7 6 5 4 3 2 1

Printed in the United States of America.

Contents

CONTENTS

Exhibits

Chapter 1

Introduction

Family Business Leadership
Is a Unique Proposition

Loretta, a daughter who succeeded her father as the CEO of the family's business, has tried to emulate his decisive, autocratic way of running things. After all, wasn't it his style of leadership that made the business the success it is today? But instead of moving forward, the business seems to be going sideways. Some of the key employees seem frustrated, and Loretta's siblings act resentful and spiteful. Her brother, a co-owner, recently snapped at her. "You think you're Dad just because you got his title?" he said. "Well, let me tell you something. You may try to imitate him but that doesn't mean you *are* him."

"In some ways, Dad had it easier," Loretta thinks. "He was the founder and the only owner. People did what he said, without question. And he didn't have any shareholders to second-guess him."

Leading any business is difficult. But leadership in a family business is a far different challenge than leadership in any other kind of business. That's because family firms are more complicated. In other businesses, a leader is concerned with only one system: the business organization. However, family firms are unique in that they involve three systems: the business, the family, and the ownership. All three systems are interrelated and interdependent, and each is in need of its own leadership.

Furthermore, leadership becomes more difficult with each succeeding generation as the family and the business grow larger and more complex and as the number of owners, often all related to each other, increases as well.

This book is aimed at helping business-owning families understand and implement the extra dimensions of leadership that family firms require. It will be especially useful to you if you have leadership responsibilities in a business-owning family or in the business itself, if you are parents preparing the next generation for leadership, or if you are among those who aspire to leadership. Others who will find this book helpful include non-family executives in a family firm, family business advisors, and family members and owners not in overt positions of leadership but who may nonetheless provide informal leadership or offer support to leaders by being good followers.

What is leadership anyway? In our view, **leadership means the ability to create a way to move forward, and to be able to inspire others to follow a designated path.** The capacity for stimulating movement in a particular direction is another way to define it. It does not always involve moving an organization toward that goal. Sometimes leadership is required before you even have a goal, and leadership may be provided in the direction of determining a goal.

Leadership, as we see it, is about action, and so this book is about action. It is focused on making things happen and getting things done—"pulling the trigger" of actually leading. Although two chapters address preparation for leadership, this book as a whole is less concerned with developing the potential to lead than with the process of leadership itself and ways to improve it. In a sense, this is a how-to book aimed at helping people exercise effective leadership in family businesses and in business-owning families.

As a reader, you can expect to gain three important things from this book:

1. Appreciation for the fact that different people have different gifts and abilities and therefore what works for one leader may not work for another.

2. Recognition that business environments change and leadership must be prepared to respond to those changes.
3. An understanding that families and ownership structures also change over time and leadership must be able to meet the needs that such changes present.

You will also learn how the demands of family business leadership differ from those of non-family businesses. You will be given tools for sharpening your leadership skills and, if you are at the point of beginning your career, you will find tips and strategies for gaining the credibility you need to put yourself on the path to leadership.

As you read these pages, you will also discover how crisis presents opportunity for leadership, how some people lead without appearing to lead at all, and how to earn the right to lead. And, you will learn ways to overcome many of the impediments to leadership. (Sometimes the biggest impediment is you!)

If your family's business has been successful, it's only natural to want to continue and build on that success. It may be tempting to continue to do things as they were done in the past because that's what built the success in the first place. However, success in the past does not guarantee success in the future. As the business environment changes and as the family and ownership structures change with each new generation, leadership, to be effective, must also change. This does not mean that "change for the sake of change" is effective leadership. The ability to "hold a course in turbulent times" can also be a sign of successful leadership. But we must acknowledge that change is the primary challenge faced by all leaders.

Success in the past does not guarantee success in the future.

Chapter 2

Wanted

An Assortment of Able Leaders

People tend to focus a lot of attention on succession in a family business—that is, who in the next generation will succeed to the top leadership position. This is important, but it can be too narrow a focus, especially if being named the successor CEO is viewed as "THE prize" and the CEO is venerated more than other family members.

The fact is that, unless a family opts to have a team of co-CEOs, only one person can become the chief executive in a business. Fortunately, however, where family businesses are concerned, there are many other extremely significant opportunities for leadership.

You are probably already familiar with the three-circle model of family business shown in Exhibit 1.[1] This widely used model illustrates family business as three overlapping systems—the business, the family, and ownership. People can fit into any one of these systems or into all three. You might be a family member but not a shareholder or an employee of the business. Or you might be both an owner and a family member but not work in the business. You might be a non-family executive in the business and also own a small stake in the company. One of the great features of this model is that it demonstrates how complicated life can be in a family business or business-owning family. If, you are in the center segment—meaning you are a family member and

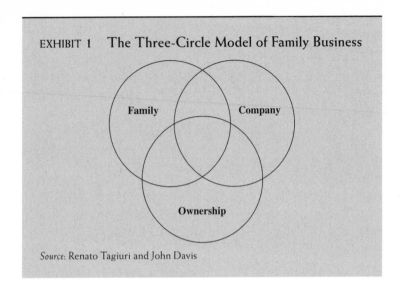

EXHIBIT 1   The Three-Circle Model of Family Business

Family

Company

Ownership

Source: Renato Tagiuri and John Davis

an owner and you work in the business—you will find yourself playing many roles. Sometimes you will be asking yourself which is the appropriate role in a given situation. "Do I act as an uncle here? Or as my niece's boss?" The model can help you focus on the proper role.

Particularly relevant to the topic of this book, however, is that the circles make it clear that **there are three systems needing leadership talent, not just the business. The ownership system and the family also need good leaders**. Let's take each system one by one:

THE BUSINESS

The business needs a CEO and other senior executives to develop strategy and move the business forward. Leadership in the family business requires knowledge, experience, good judgment, interpersonal skill, and credibility as they relate to the business and business decisions.

As generations progress in family businesses, leadership becomes a team approach with no one saying, "I am the boss and you will do what I tell you to do." Instead, a group of siblings or cousins says, "We are a team of executives. Each of us is here not because of our last name or because of who our grandfather was, but because we have prepared ourselves to be here, because we're motivated to be here, and because we bring skills and talents representing specific disciplines within the world of business. We have worked together to develop a common vision and a common strategy and we are working together to implement that in the best possible way for the benefit of all our constituencies."

With such a team, one family member might be CEO, another might be CFO, and still another might be a senior vice president heading up sales or production. The executive team is likely to also include key non-family executives. Critical to their success as a leadership team are their credibility—based on knowledge, skill, and experience—and their commitment to leading for the benefit of all involved, not just for themselves.

Although the words "leadership" and "management" are often used interchangeably, we believe there are some important differences. Leadership needs to be focused primarily on vision and on strategy that will fulfill or attain the vision. As we said in the introduction, **leadership means creating a way to move forward.**

Leadership in the family business requires knowledge, experience, good judgment, interpersonal skill, and credibility.

Leadership needs to be focused primarily on vision and on strategy that will fulfill or attain the vision.

Management is more concerned with implementing tasks that need to be done. It is more about control. It implies organization; leadership does not. Leadership can be messy and chaotic.

It is a rare and wonderful manager who also has leadership capabilities. Managers can be leaders and leaders can be managers, but the two abilities don't necessarily go together.

For the sake of simplicity, however, we'll use the term "management" when we're referring to the running of the business.

THE FAMILY

Often overlooked is the fact that the family needs leadership too—not just a "head of the family" but multiple leaders who can focus on meeting the family's needs as a family. Moving the family forward as a cohesive unit that gives management and the business the vital support they need is a key function. The family provides many rich opportunities for leadership, especially for family members who have talent, who wish to be involved in the family, and who wish to maintain a meaningful link to the business without actually working in it.

Family leaders play roles that run parallel to those of business leaders. If you're in business leadership, your role is to advance the business. If you're in family leadership, your goal is to advance the family. Family leaders build family unity by nurturing relationships among family members. As the family moves into the second, third, and fourth generations, family leaders frequently articulate the shared values of the family. In so doing, they create opportunities to build and display the family's culture—its belief in philanthropy, or its commitment to do good in the community. Family leaders also deal with and help resolve family conflicts and family crises.

In family businesses, family leadership is often informal and unrecognized. Even though it is often perceived that the business leader is also the family leader in the first generation, the reality is usually somewhat different. The founder, typically male, focuses mainly on the business and on providing opportunity and wealth for the family, while his wife, though she may have duties in the business, concentrates primarily on the family and maintaining relationships among its members.

Family leaders build family unity by nurturing relationships among family members.

There's no law that says the individual who serves as the business leader also has to serve as the family leader. In fact, it's probably better if separate people fill these roles. In the second generation, one sibling may rise to leadership of the family while another is viewed as the leader of the business. As the business and family expand, the family may establish a more formal family council with specifically designated leadership. The family council deals with the many issues of the family as *separate from* the business but also of the family in its *relation to* the business, such as developing a policy governing the employment of family members or a family mission statement. Committees and task forces may evolve. The family may establish a family office to manage its investments, or create a family foundation to oversee its philanthropy. The family should hold regular family meetings that deal with issues of the business and family but also give family members an opportunity to have fun together, cementing their relationships. Family meetings strengthen family members' perceptions of themselves as a family, and wise leaders will see to it that such gatherings are funded in a way that does not pose an undue financial burden on some family members.

Many business-owning families focus their attention on the transition of leadership in the business without thinking of what will happen in the family when the current family leaders are no longer present. For example, will the siblings continue to value family relationships when Mom and Dad are no longer around? Will the family business continue to benefit from family unity? Whether in support of family or of business, family unity requires good family leadership.

Too often, in our experience, people in the family system go along for the ride instead of stepping up and providing leadership. Yet it's incredibly important for virtually everyone in the business-owning family to be looking for opportunities to make contributions. When family members seek opportunities, they usually appear.

Suppose, for example, that you accept an assignment to serve on a committee to develop policies about the employment of next-generation family members in the business. You may not be the CEO of the business, family council chairman, or even head of the committee. **Nevertheless, if you take your role seriously and take an active part in the committee's work, you have a tremendous opportunity to be a constructive force in the family for generations to come.** Your actions may include doing thorough research, or visiting other family businesses to gather valuable information. That's leadership, too.

At almost any family meeting, you'll have an opportunity to provide leadership by saying, "Here's an issue that we need to deal with." When you pay attention, make yourself knowledgeable, prepare yourself to be able to recognize opportunities, say something when an opportunity presents itself, and are prepared to invest the time, effort, and energy to resolve the issue, you are providing family leadership.

We have known family leaders, often members of the senior generation, who because of their experience and credibility take on difficult and sometimes thankless tasks because they know it will help the current or next generation succeed. This "Servant Leadership" often occurs without titles or other forms of personal acknowledgment in families.

OWNERSHIP

The ownership system needs leaders in the form of a chairman of the board and other directors who bring the needs of all three systems together and who guide the business in accordance with the wishes of the owners and the values of the family. What board leadership does is move the assets of the family forward in relation to moving the family forward. It has a foot in each of the other two arenas—family and business—and needs to have a great deal of understanding about both of those systems. On the family side, the board's leadership should be related more to the values and the goals of the family for the business rather than on relationships within the family. On the business side, it means translating family goals and values into forms that allow holding management accountable for performance that represents the best interests of the owners.

We have often said that chairman of the board is a real job and a real leadership challenge. It shouldn't be used as a means of putting an aging CEO out to pasture. Frequently, family businesses combine the roles of chairman and CEO, but we think there is wisdom in separating the two responsibilities. For one thing, the CEO already has his or her hands full running the business. A separate individual serving as chairman can give full attention to the leadership of an active board representing the interests of owners in a way that a CEO cannot.

What do boards do? As stated in *Letting Go: Preparing Yourself to Relinquish Control of the Family Business*, "An excellent board provides strategic oversight, evaluates corporate and top-executive performance, represents and relates with shareholders, serves as a resource to top management, protects and enhances the company's assets, and fulfills legal requirements."[2] Ideally, a board will not only consist of some key family members but will also include at least two or three talented business leaders from outside the family and its business.

One of the most valuable leadership roles the chairman and the board can play is to build shareholder loyalty, awareness, and cooperation and to encourage the notion of "patient capital"— the family owners' willingness to leave their funds invested in the company so that long-term business goals can be met. To be successful, ownership leaders must stay in tune with what shareholders are thinking, what they see as important, and what their needs are.

In one unfortunate situation, a second-generation CEO we'll call Jarvis ran the business as if it were his, failing to take into consideration the needs and desires of the two nieces and a nephew, all in their twenties, who had inherited shares from their deceased father (Jarvis's brother). Jarvis also chaired the board, which was made up of family members—his two sisters and his mother—who tended to go along with what Jarvis wanted.

Jarvis deprived the third-generation shareholders of information about the business, implying that they were not capable of understanding it. And, because they were not on the board, they had no part in the decision making. They received only a trickle in dividends. None of the third-generation worked in the business.

Understandably, these young shareholders grew more and more frustrated and began to make a fuss. "What are you doing with our inheritance?" they asked their uncle. "Why aren't we getting more money out of this?" They began to badger their aunts and grandmother until finally, there was so much rancor that the only thing family members could agree on was to sell the business. And that was a shame, because the business had been very successful and Jarvis had actually done a good job of running it.

What Jarvis had failed to understand was that the business was not just *his*. It belonged to his nieces and nephew as well as to the other shareholders. Jarvis didn't understand that if you can't recognize the legitimacy of the rest of the owners, you're not going to be a fully effective leader because they won't believe that you have their best interest at heart.

So, ownership needs good leadership and, again, there are many opportunities. Being a director is, in itself, a leadership role. The board needs other officers and committee chairs. Becoming more common on boards is the role of "lead director," who is empowered to convene meetings of the board without the chairman and/or CEO being present. When an individual is both chairman and CEO, the lead director leads those meetings where the CEO's performance is being evaluated. He or she also runs the board when there's a potential conflict of interest for the chairman to do so.

EXHIBIT 2 **The Many Opportunities for Leadership**

Business	Family	Ownership
Leadership role:	*Leadership role:*	*Leadership role:*
To develop strategy and move the business forward.	To meet the family's needs as a family and to move it forward as a cohesive unit that supports the business.	To bring the needs of all three groups together and to guide the business.
Leadership opportunities:	*Leadership opportunities:*	*Leadership opportunities:*
CEO President	Family council chair or other officer	Chairman of the board or other officer
COO CFO	Committee chair Task force chair	Lead director Executive committee member
CIO	Family office chair or other officer	Committee chair
Executive vice president Senior vice president Division head	Family foundation chair or other officer	Task force chair Director

OTHER WAYS LEADERSHIP DIFFERS IN FAMILY FIRMS

The fact that family businesses need leaders in three co-existing systems is only one way that leadership in family firms differs from that of other companies. While emotion is always a factor in any business, the fact that family is involved in family firms means that their leaders will have to deal with emotion, to a much greater extent because family members tend to have passionate feelings—positive and negative—about the business. Trust and loyalty are also more significant issues in family companies. In our experience, trust is the currency of family business leadership, and leaders' success depends significantly on their ability to perform in ways that build trust. Any behavior that adds to the leader's "bank account" of trust makes him or her stronger, but any that subtracts from that bank account makes the leader weaker. Actions perceived by others as self-serving, for example, tend to subtract from a leader's trust balance.

Trust is the currency of family business leadership, and leaders' success depends significantly on their ability to perform in ways that build trust.

Another difference is that in a publicly traded corporation, an executive's job is to increase shareholder value. Family business owners, however, have multiple goals. Owners want to increase shareholder value, but as family members, they may also want to pass the asset on to the next generation, provide employment for the next generation, transmit the family's values through the business to its employees and the community, create a name for the family, and meet charitable goals. Needless to say, it is easier to lead toward a single, very specific goal like increasing shareholder value than it is to have to weigh a number of goals simultaneously and provide leadership toward their achievement.

LEADING CULTURE AND VALUES

Culture, values, and legacy are important to all businesses, but nowhere are they more important than in family-owned companies. Being consistent with the culture and the values of the family and its business and a recognition of the reverence with which families often regard businesses that have been handed down from generation to generation are essential dimensions of family business leadership. The most successful family business leaders strike a critical balance between being respectful of the past without being immobilized by loyalty to what went before.

Leading culture and values means articulating vision, and this in turn means not only stating business goals but also communicating beliefs and values in a way that builds cohesiveness and motivation in both business and family. The CEO who understands this not only does what must be done to make the business successful but also reinforces and assures that the culture defined by the family is part of what drives the business as a whole.

In one business, family tradition mandated that family employees were on the loading dock from the first day in the business, interacting with the employees, learning to speak their language about a variety of subjects. Family members took their turns on midnight shifts and showed they weren't afraid of hard, physical labor. They demonstrated that they were *of* the people and that they understood that the family was successful because of the people who worked with them. They valued their employees and honored a culture that said, "We're a team and we work very hard to make sure that everybody benefits." As a result, when a recession hit, the family was quickly able to implement changes that gave the company a huge competitive advantage over competitors with less constructive employee relations.

In another situation, family dissension during a business downturn began to contribute to further deterioration for a fifth-generation firm we'll call Hale Brothers Brewery. Many of the nearly 100 family shareholders were dependent on the company dividends and grew fearful and agitated when the dividends were decreased. Others became angry when, for the first time, the company was forced to lay off a large number of employees. The well-being of the employees and of the community in which Hale Brothers was located were among the values the family had always held dear. One cousin challenged Ellis Hale, the incumbent CEO, on his leadership and sought the job for himself. Ultimately, Ellis was backed by the board, enabling him to move the company in some new directions—including introducing light, non-alcoholic, and low-carb beers and entering new geographic markets, not only with its own products but also by acquiring a number of successful microbreweries.

Ellis recognized that his board of directors had been so distracted by the family issues that it couldn't really focus on what needed to be done in the business. He was determined to move family dynamics out of the board room. To accomplish that, he worked with a family business consultant to set up a family council with its own leadership. The council was permitted to elect one member to the company board to represent the goals and values of the family. As Ellis puts it, "The family has a vote but not a veto on our company board of directors." That meant the family business would always take into consideration its past and would respect the family's values, but that it would also constantly re-evaluate, re-interpret, and update what both the business and the family were about.

Throughout the long, arduous effort of turning the company around, Ellis said to himself again and again, "I have to make all aspects of this company profitable, but I have to do it in ways that are considerate of the family and its traditions." A tremendous communicator, he wrote long, articulate letters to the board, to the shareholders, and to the employees, and he worked to build coalitions around the actions that were necessary. Ultimately, he was successful at putting the company on its feet again and convincing the family that the decision to retain him as CEO had been the right one.

MINDING YOUR CHECKS AND BALANCES

Leadership, like any type of power, is potentially dangerous and needs to be treated like live ammunition. Leadership can get out of control. It can be corrupted. Individuals who exercise it can be overcome by their own emotions or ambitions and can lead a company to destruction rather than success. Particularly, in today's business environment, trust is a precious commodity. The most significant criterion for establishing trust in a business relationship is a leader's reputation for ethics. In a family business, values are the bond of trust that holds the family and the business together and they must be modeled by leaders.

Consider the once-proud family-controlled Pennsylvania cable company, Adelphia. Adelphia's founder, John Rigas, and his son Timothy were convicted of multiple counts of fraud, looting their company for personal gain and misleading investors.

Sometimes in a family business, individuals equate power with leadership. If they own the majority of shares, they may believe they have the right to do as they please—rewarding themselves more than is proper, or riding roughshod over the ideas, desires, and values of other shareholders, family members, and employees.

Fortunately, family businesses have or can create moderating influences to channel power and leadership in constructive ways. An active board of directors, family councils, family mission and value statements, and family business policies all serve as checks on family business leadership. They function somewhat like the United States government, with its legislative, executive, and judicial branches all offsetting one another through a balance of power.

We know of two brothers who confused power with leadership. Together, they controlled the family company's voting stock and, because they did, they assumed that they had the capacity to lead. But their cousins, the minority shareholders, knew neither of the brothers was capable of leadership and they rose up as a unified group and said, "Neither of you can be president. And if you don't listen to us, we'll go to court and claim that you're violating your fiduciary responsibility by not creating a board that provides the leadership that's necessary to make this company work." The cousins placed an effective check on the irresponsible and arrogant brothers. Now the family as a whole is working on defusing its "bombs"—the brothers' power as majority owners and the cousins' threat of legal action.

An active board of directors, family councils, family mission and value statements, and family business policies all serve as checks on family business leadership.

As you can see, leadership in a family business does not reside in just one individual. Because a family business consists of three intertwined systems, it needs many good leaders at many levels. If you look for them, you'll find many opportunities for providing leadership. And they will be interesting opportunities that will give you a chance to stretch and grow and to earn the respect of those around you in the family and in the business. The challenges and demands are many, and we talk more about them in the next chapter.

Chapter 3

Understanding the Demands of Leadership

When Anil Nanji assumed top leadership of Magnet Sales & Manufacturing, Inc., on his father's death, he found he could not adopt his father's style of leadership. He admired his father. "He was a very dynamic person, very energetic, very committed, and actually a very good role model in many ways because he was very much on the straight and narrow. He always had a lot of integrity," Nanji told *Nation's Business* magazine.

Yet, he saw his parent as a hard-driving "Type A" personality, one who was often erratic. "Things could change on a whim—his whim," said Nanji. The elder Nanji also tended to inspire fear among the employees of the Culver City, California, magnet fabricator.

Not only was Anil Nanji a different person from his father, but the world had changed. In the early 1980s, he recalled, employees were told what to do and given a lot of guidance. By the mid 1990s, however, when Nanji took over, the emergence of new technology and a new kind of workforce, one that was more "internally driven," he said, required a different kind of leadership. Nanji set about to shape a different working climate, one in which the goals are communicated to the employees and they "figure out for themselves how to get there," he said.

"I think the most valuable thing that we have is energy and spirit," Nanji said. "It's my job to try to create an environment in which these can flourish and these can be unleashed."[3]

What Anil Nanji understood is that **a change in leadership means change.** Unfortunately, most business-owning families fall into a leadership trap in which Dad has been the primary leadership role model, his style of leadership has been successful, and, since the family wants to continue the business's success, Junior is expected to lead the company just like Dad did. But the reality is, Junior can't do that, nor should he try. Even when parents have done an outstanding job of leading the family business, it is important to recognize that the next generation cannot and should not lead in the same way. For three reasons:

1. Children are different people from their parents and do not have the exact same gifts and abilities. What works for one as a leader may not work for another.
2. Business environments change, and leadership must be prepared to respond accordingly, regardless of what has proven successful in the past.
3. Families and ownership structures change and leadership must be relevant for their needs.

In this chapter, we want to focus on each stage of the family business and how each generation differs in terms of the leadership challenges it faces. We will also introduce four leadership styles and describe the circumstances in which each is the most effective.

FOUR STYLES OF LEADERSHIP

Let's begin by looking at what we see as the four styles of leadership. Then we will show you how they relate to the stages of a family business.

Directing

A Directing leader gives specific instructions to followers and provides direct, close supervision. He's not keen on employees doing things their own way. Nobody works in the business unless they take direction from him. He makes all the decisions and tends not to seek much input from others.

A Directing style is best suited to businesses that are startups and that are owned and managed by one individual. However, a Directing style also works effectively in other generations of a family business under certain circumstances—when there's an emergency, when a business is in a turnaround survival mode, during periods of rapid and significant change, or when there is a low level of trust in an organization. A Directing leader is the kind of leader needed when there is a lack of confidence in the team, and when employees are inexperienced or have limited competence. Outstanding employees, however, are unlikely to stick around if they're always being told what to do.

Coaching

The Coaching leader focuses on the future, not just what needs to be done right now. With the future in mind, this leader wants to develop the members of the group and the group as a whole. He or she is a person who is able to see the unique abilities that each member brings to the group, and appreciates that the group together has more strength than any one individual. Coaching leaders serve as mentors and teachers, and they gain their credibility and right to lead by helping others succeed and grow.

Coaching leaders are transformational leaders. They embrace change and they help others embrace change as well. One of their great strengths in a family business is preparing the next generation for leadership.

This style of leadership is especially appropriate when the future of the business is the focus, transfer of ownership and development of future leaders are the goals, and cultural change is needed but change is not time-critical (as it would be in an emergency situation or a business turnaround).

Coaching leaders are transformational leaders.

The danger of this style is that Coaching leaders can become too paternalistic or maternalistic in their approach and begin to see the employees developing as their children—an inappropriate approach even when they are.

Counseling

A Counseling leader sees when others—such as a team of sibling owners or a group of non-family executives—have the ability to take on some leadership of their own and are looking for an opportunity to exercise it. The Counseling leader helps them find those opportunities and assists them in thinking things through. When others are posing potential solutions to a problem, this leader says, "Okay, tell me more about that," and leads others through a series of questions to the point where they are able to see whether or not their proposal is a sound one. The Counselor is a "guide on the side," someone who is willing and able to give others encouragement and who helps them test their own ability, analyses, and their own ideas and decisions.

The Counseling leader is strategic.

Where the Counseling leader is transformational, the Counseling leader is strategic, taking a look at the big picture and asking the questions that keep others focused on the organization's goals. "Let's remember that what we're trying to do here is to reach a 5 percent growth in our market share this year. How will launching that new product do that? Will it take resources away from other vital areas?"

Counseling leaders can be particularly effective in a business environment where innovation and flexibility are valued, the work is technical and complex, and objectives are clearly achievable. In all likelihood, there's an ownership transfer plan in place, the next-generation leader has been chosen or the selection process is taking place, and the younger generation is motivated to lead. In addition, there's an experienced management team and a low resistance to change.

The drawback of the Counseling leader is that he or she might be seen as indecisive. When a business and a family have been headed by a Directing leader, a Counseling leader can drive people to distraction—they have been accustomed to and took great comfort in the knowledge that there was an "all-knowing, all-powerful" leader who would decide. Now they have this leader who keeps asking questions! Often the transformational leadership of a Coach is needed before a group is ready for a Counseling leader.

Delegating

The Delegating leader is a visionary leader who imagines what the possibilities are and relies on the team to do what's necessary to achieve the goals. Such leaders are disinclined to think issues through with their people. Instead, a Delegating leader wants others to take independent action, get things done, and not keep coming back for blessings. He or she trusts the team and believes decisions are best made at the point where the work takes place.

The Delegating leader is a visionary leader.

This leadership style functions most effectively in an environment where people feel secure and have a good understanding of what they are trying to accomplish. Most likely, this is a sibling- or cousin-generation business with a sound business plan and a team of experienced managers. The workforce is made up of highly competent people who have the ability to see how continuous improvements can be made. The next-generation leaders are in place, along with an experienced management team, and the culture is entrepreneurial in nature.

While a Delegating leader can "empower" others to reach their true potential both personally and for the business, this style can create paralysis if the manager or group is not ready. Often, the challenge is to know when to Delegate and when circumstances call for a Counseling or even Coaching approach.

If there's a danger to being a Delegating leader, it might be that sometimes when he or she tells someone to "sink or swim," the individual might not be prepared to swim. And again, like Counseling leaders, Delegating leaders may sometimes be seen as indecisive.

Which Leadership Style Is Best?

The answer to this question is—it all depends. It depends upon the leader, the needs of the people being led, and the business environment itself. It is important to understand that these four "styles of leadership" represent a range of options from which an effective leader may choose. The best leaders are those who develop the skills to employ a range of options that will allow them to respond to the needs of the business and the family at any given moment in their continuous development. An effective leader may need to be a Coach to some while Counseling others and Delegating to those who are ready.

Founding-Generation Leadership

People who start businesses are often uniquely gifted individuals who take an idea and transform it into a successful enterprise. In the early stages of a business startup, they do virtually every job and develop a profound knowledge of every aspect of their enterprise. At this stage, they are generally both sole owner and manager. Being the founder, owner, and knowledgeable manager imbues them with a "legitimate authority" that is recognized and accorded great deference throughout the organization and the family. It is important to note this because the same degree of legitimate authority will not be available to successive leaders. They will have to earn their credibility and right to lead by different means.

Entrepreneurs tend to be strong-willed, tough-minded, and dominating, because that's what it takes to start a business from scratch and to fight the odds and make things happen. Often, such personalities can be hard on others, and family members may become resentful.

The challenges of leadership that founders face include the personal discipline that they have to have to start a business and the sacrifices that they're willing to endure. Often they find themselves pushing the business to grow at the expense of their own financial well-being. They must also exert leadership to convince others—lenders, customers, suppliers, and non-family employees—to buy into their vision. In short, it takes grit and self-confidence to create something new and to make others believe you can achieve your vision.

It should come as no surprise that the founding-generation leader in a family business is, more often than not, a Directing leader. In startups and owner-managed businesses, the leader feels that "nobody knows how to do it better than I do." Directing leadership works for a while in a first-generation business. Eventually, however, in order for the business to go on, the founder needs to back away from that style somewhat and move to the Coaching style, encouraging younger family members to have an interest in the business, to think about its future, and to develop a new vision for it. A founder who persists in a dominating Directing role risks having his children feel they cannot deal with him. When that happens, they lose the desire to be a part of the business. A Directing style also makes it difficult to bring in good non-family executives.

The founder, then, needs to be able to take a different view, one that allows him to say, "Another kind of leadership is needed, but that doesn't mean my leadership style was bad."

In fact, what this leader did *was* good. His Directing style of leadership was exactly what was needed to get the business off the ground. However, it is not sufficient for the business to be healthy going into the future.

Sibling-Generation Leadership

In the second stage of a family business, when the siblings are involved, leadership needs to be team-oriented. No longer will the one-person rule that served the business under the founder be effective or even possible. Even if there's a single top leader of the business, it's essential that this CEO and all the siblings recognize that the others have a stake in the business.

> Perhaps the greatest leadership challenge in the sibling generation is to develop a vision for what the company needs to be when it comes time to make the transition to the cousin generation.

Too often, we have seen sibling-generation leaders react with disdain when their brothers and sisters raise issues about how their investment in the business is being managed. "You didn't do anything to earn this," such CEOs may say. "Mom and Dad gave it to you. You don't have a right to question." The truth is, however, that Mom and Dad gave the CEO his or her shares, too, and the other share-owning brothers and sisters do indeed have a right to question. They are all part of the team, whether they work in the business or not.

The sibling generation's need to develop a group approach to leadership is as critical to the family as it is to the business. At this stage, it becomes important for the family as a whole to make decisions about many issues, such as what the requirements will be for their children to join the business and what the code of conduct should be for family members.

Perhaps the greatest leadership challenge in the sibling generation is to develop a vision for what the company needs to be when it comes time to make the transition to the cousin generation. The siblings will need to go beyond the founder's vision, which was limited by his own experience and expertise, and think in terms of business continuity. That means leaders in the second generation giving thought to and engaging in planning about such questions as: What size does this business need to be in order to be truly competitive in this marketplace? How large does it need to be to be responsive to family needs? Is this even the business we should be in?

In essence, the sibling team should be able to say, "We've inherited a great legacy, but it's up to us to take it to the next level." This is the stage of a family business when Coaching and Counseling emerge as the appropriate leadership styles, and leaders can move back and forth among them as necessary. However, if leadership has decided that a drastic change is in order—moving out of the present line of business and into another, then a return to a Directing style may be in order. Or, as second-generation leadership is thinking about how the family's growing business is going to need others in significant leadership roles, it will mean Delegating leadership responsibility. The leader still establishes the vision, but relies on others to accomplish its realization.

Cousin-Generation Leadership

In the cousin stage and beyond, family business leadership becomes a matter of pulling together and inspiring people who are, in many ways, only loosely related. They are people who have grown up in very different households and may live in vastly different parts of the country or the world. They probably only have an interest in the business because they still share the same name or because they have some sort of financial interest in it. The business by now is more professionalized and, in some ways, run much more like a public corporation.

Leadership at this stage requires an emphasis on communication to keep diverse and far-flung family members and shareholders informed, involved, and cohesive. Visionary leaders can be particularly important now in articulating what the business has meant to the family and its heritage, in expressing clearly the values and the mission of the business and the family, and in demonstrating how it all works together.

A special challenge to leadership now is to direct attention to the needs and perspective of the shareholders. In the founder and sibling generations, when the business and the family were smaller, it made more sense for the family to make sacrifices for the growth of the business. It was more likely to be seen as "Dad's business" or "our business." A greater proportion of family members were working in the business, profits were re-invested in it, and family members received extrinsic rewards in the form of salaries or perks.

A leader needs to be someone that the share-holders believe has their best interest at heart.

By the cousin stage, however, not everyone can or wants to work in the business, and family shareholders are looking for reasons why they should remain invested in the family firm. Leadership must find a way to balance the shareholders' legitimate right to extrinsic rewards in the form of distributions or dividends with the need to re-invest profits into the business so that it can grow and provide greater returns in the future. A leader now needs to be someone that the shareholders believe has their best interest at heart. He or she needs to be able to craft a vision that will inspire their commitment to the business. That will include being able to articulate and promote the intrinsic rewards that the business offers in terms of the family's values, their place in the community, and the asset that is being built for future generations of family members. In summary, the leader needs to be concerned with creating an overarching process for developing among present and future family shareholders an understanding of the realities of ownership and its rights and responsibilities.

Excellent leadership in this generation will be characterized by communication skills and the ability to educate others. The leader has to be prepared to use all four styles of leadership as appropriate, but needs to focus particularly on the Coaching and Counseling aspects of developing future generations of ownership and leadership.

INTEGRATING THE PIECES

Give some attention to Exhibit 3 below and you will see how the four leadership styles fit in each stage of a family business, the business environment, and the family environment. You can refer to this exhibit time and again to refresh your thinking about what leadership style to employ in any given situation.

Also, you may be more familiar with thinking of leadership in terms of a spectrum, ranging from "autocratic" to "participative." It may be helpful to think of the Directing style as autocratic and Coaching, Counseling, and Delegating as progressively participative.

EXHIBIT 3   Leadership Styles for Family Business

Business Environment	Style	Family & Organization Environment
• Startup—new business concept • Owner-managed • Turnaround survival mode • Rapid, significant change • Low trust level	**Directing Leader** • Hands-on • Provides specific instructions to followers— obvious expertise • Direct/close supervision	• First-generation family • Inexperienced employees • Lack of confidence in team • Limited competence of workers
• Transfer of ownership goal • Future is the focus • Change is not time critical • Development is the goal • Culture change is needed	**Coaching Leader** • Transformational • Focus on personal and team development of others • Teacher/mentor	• Respect for leader's expertise is widespread • Skilled workers who need development • Next-generation leadership preparation

Continued

EXHIBIT 3   Continued

Business Environment	Style	Family & Organization Environment
• Ownership transfer plan in place • Multiple owners and generations • Innovation and flexibility valued • Technical and complex work • Objectives are clearly achievable	**Counseling Leader** • Strategic • Focus on big-picture issues • Goal oriented	• Next-generation leader(s) chosen and motivated to lead • Experienced management team • Technical skills in followers • Low resistance to change
• Sibling team/ cousins ownership • Sustainable competitive advantage • Continuous improvement process	**Delegating Leader** • Visionary • Trust in leadership team	• Next-generation leader(s) in place • Experienced management team • Entrepreneurial culture

THE ART OF DELEGATION

A few more words about Delegating are in order. It's likely to be the style that the next generation in a family business didn't see much of in the previous generation, particularly when it's a first-to-second-generation transition. So we want to say to current leaders: "To develop the younger generation, you need to begin developing your own Delegating style as a leader." When incumbent leaders learn to delegate, it accomplishes two things: (1) It helps shift the opportunity to lead and to learn about leadership to the next generation, and (2) it also helps the next generation to see a different model of how to lead.

Delegating means giving up that very thing you would often like to hold on to most—authority— while retaining the thing you would most like to give up—responsibility.

We have found, however, that Directing leaders often don't really understand delegation and make some mistakes as they try to move into this style. **Delegating is not the indiscriminate dumping of work assignments on other people. Nor is it giving orders.**

True Delegating means the leader is confident of the follower's maturity, or readiness, to handle the task and makes sure he or she fully understands the objectives. The Delegating leader also gives that person the authority to accomplish what is assigned.

We're sorry to say it, but some CEOs believe they are delegating to others when what they are really doing is preserving their own image as the hero-CEO. They do this when they give assignments just to show how difficult their own role is and how good they are. They may deprive the individual, inadvertently or deliberately, of insight and knowledge they have gained that would help the younger person accomplish the task in question. In other words, they set up the younger person to fail. Then they excuse themselves by saying, "Well, you know, I had to learn it the hard way."

While it's true that everybody has to learn certain things by experience, a **good Delegating leader tries to prepare the person to whom the task will be given.** If an individual is not prepared, the leader sees that some Counseling or Coaching may be in order before an assignment is made.

When you're an effective Delegating leader, you also know that true Delegating means giving up that very thing you would often like to hold on to most—authority—while retaining the

EXHIBIT 4   What Delegating Means

1. Choosing the right person for the task—one who is capable and prepared.
2. Explaining the objectives and making sure they're understood.
3. Seeing to it that the individual has all the information needed. Is there knowledge or insight that you can share from your own experience? Are there facts he or she needs to know?
4. Giving the individual the authority to do the job.
5. Letting the individual find his or her own way to complete the assignment.
6. As the leader, retaining accountability.

thing you would most like to give up—responsibility. While your follower is responsible to you for carrying out the assignment, you know that when you're the leader, you remain ultimately accountable.

When the current leader is comfortable with four different styles instead of being limited to one, he or she can provide the next generation with different models of leadership and help them to see that there is no one "correct" style. That's an enormous gift to younger family members, who might otherwise feel compelled to lead "just like Mom" or "just like Dad."

Although this chapter has focused largely on the business system to demonstrate its points, the four leadership styles apply to the family and ownership systems as well. Family leaders and board leaders alike will benefit from familiarizing themselves with the four styles and understanding more about the needs of leadership of each stage of the family business.

Chapter 4

What Makes Leaders Effective?

A s the previous chapter suggests, there is no one "sure" style of leadership, and no single leader can serve as a model for everyone. Instead, there are many great leaders to draw on. Their examples can inspire you to adapt the four styles of leadership to your own skills and personality. We are deliberate in saying "styles," plural, because we believe effective leadership is situational. That is, it changes with the situation, whether the situation is a first-, second-, or third-generation company, a business in crisis, a business that has plateaued, a small business, a startup, or an established company, an experienced workforce or an inexperienced one. Instead of relying on one style, **outstanding leaders develop the ability to use all four styles of leadership and choose the best one for the circumstances.**

Within the four basic styles of leadership you have been introduced to, there are many variations, depending on a leader's gifts and personality. Some leaders are charismatic—they excite one's imagination, ignite passion, and inspire devotion to a cause. They are often transformational leaders, bringing about great change in a business, a family, or whatever it is they lead. Others are steady hands on the wheel. Without fanfare, they move a company or organization along. In a family business, just because the guy who's destined to succeed Mom is really dull and boring doesn't mean he's going to be a bad leader. He may be just what the family and the business need right now.

A good example of such contrasts is Malcolm S. Forbes and his older brother, Bruce. Bruce succeeded his father as the president of *Forbes* magazine and ran it for ten years. "Compared with Malcolm, Bruce had modest ambitions: he simply wanted *Forbes* to flourish," observes Malcolm's biographer, Christopher Winans.[4] Under Bruce's leadership, the circulation tripled and the magazine gained credibility and stature. Winans credits Brace's congeniality and salesmanship with putting *Forbes* "on a path of dynamic growth."[5] But it was the once-quiet, intellectual Malcolm who had big ideas and big ambitions. After Bruce died and Malcolm inherited the mantle of *Forbes* leadership, he propelled the company into a media empire and himself into worldwide celebrity. Each was the right leader for the time.

WHAT LEADERSHIP IS . . . AND IS NOT

To understand what makes leadership effective, it helps to understand what leadership is not. It is not just holding a position and having a title. Just "being there" is not leadership. Nor is leadership a "type" of personality. It is not self-interested—that is, it doesn't seek to satisfy the leader's own goals and desires. It does not mean talking *to* people or insisting on respect. It also does not mean simply issuing commands. One company president had a talented but particularly bossy department head. "Dorothy," he counseled her, "everybody knows you're the boss. You don't have to act like one."

The Paradox of Influence

Leadership is fundamentally about the ability to influence others. Real leaders have influence even if they don't have legitimate power or position authority. But to be an effective leader you must also be open to being influenced. People whom you want to influence are most likely to be open to your leadership if they feel they can also influence you. We all know that we trust the leadership of those we feel are most knowledgeable about our own needs—in other words, those who have been open to our influence. **Fundamentally, "... influence over others is purchased at the price of allowing one's self to be influenced by others ..."**

Leadership is fundamentally about the ability to influence others.

The best leaders share many common characteristics, no matter what styles they employ. The following have our vote as some of the most critical factors that constitute effective leaders:

♦ **They derive their power from their ability to define the issues or define the moment and to do so consistent with the values and perceptions of the group that they are leading.** Having defined the moment, they provide a model of exemplary behavior—they do what's right as perceived by the group that they are attempting to lead.

♦ **They give shape to the group's goals and values.** Often, groups haven't defined what they want. An effective leader listens very hard and gathers information over a period of time and then expresses what he's heard as the collective desire. It may seem like he is coming up with this statement himself, but he is really drawing on the information he has gathered and is processing it in a creative way. If what he does seems right, people in the group will say, "Yeah! That's it! Let's go!"

The leader then essentially pledges, "We're going to do everything consistent with what it is you've stated." He will spend a lot of time communicating why and how the decisions that are reached are consistent with the values and goals that have been articulated.

◆ **Effective leaders know that the position they hold is not in itself leadership.** They understand that what the position gives them is the permission, the credibility, and the opportunity to exercise leadership and move an organization toward its goals.

◆ **They recognize opportunity for leadership.** Oftentimes, opportunities arrive in the guise of disasters or crises, but effective leaders rise up to meet challenging circumstances.

A non-family CEO we'll call Roberto comes to mind. Roberto was hired by a fractious family that owned Chicken Plus, a fast-food chain with more than 300 franchise outlets across the country. Now in its third generation, the company is divided among 30 or so shareholders, with three cousins together owning a majority of the stock. Roberto had been a successful second-in-command in a much larger fast-food company and was looking forward to running the whole show when he joined Chicken Plus. What the family hadn't told him but what he learned during his first few days on the job was that Chicken Plus was in dire financial straits and a third of the franchisees had filed suit against it.

Undaunted, Roberto set to work. A master at dealing with the family, he personally visited all 30 family shareholders to gain an understanding of who they were, what they were hoping for, and what they thought the problems were. He visited with many of the franchisees to gain their perspective. He persuaded the family to bring in several outstanding outside board members, who were helpful in bringing objectivity and wisdom to an otherwise family-dominated board.

Roberto worked untiringly behind the scenes to build consensus on every issue that was important with whatever constituency was required—family, shareholders, board members, franchisees, vendors, and so on. And he diligently resisted the temptation, so typical of CEOs in his position, to say to his employers, "Look, I used to run a division twice the size of this company and I know what I'm doing. If you don't get out of my way, I'm not going to be your CEO anymore." What he did instead was to quietly make sure he understood the needs of his constituencies and to develop their understanding of whatever moves the company needed to make to become stable once more.

In retrospect, Roberto says, "Being confronted with that crisis was the greatest thing that could have happened to me. I understood its urgency and because I dealt with it successfully, that gave me the credibility to build and lead the company with the family's support."

Roberto exemplifies many of the hallmarks of leadership that we are talking about in this book. He had a tremendous affinity for and ability to work with the family. He not only brought credibility to his position, but he built on it by seeing a crisis as an opportunity and handling it effectively. He responded constantly to his constituencies and developed coalitions among them. And he provided education to people and explained to them why certain decisions would be in their interest.

♦ **Effective leaders are articulate.** That doesn't necessarily mean that they are great speechmakers. However, they are able to express the goals and values of the group and explain decisions and actions in terms of moving the organization toward its goals and of exemplifying its values.

♦ **They are willing to act.** In their minds, if you're not acting, you're not leading. They know there's a time for deliberation, but they also know that there's a limit to deliberation and that action must follow.

♦ **They deflect the credit to others but if there's blame to be assigned, they take the responsibility.** They follow the old saw, "There's no end to what you can get done if you don't worry about who gets the credit for it." Many of the most effective leaders are self-effacing. They concentrate on involving people and giving them the opportunity to share in the credit. They don't worry about being seen as a hero. They are concerned about getting too much recognition as a leader rather than about not getting enough.

◆ **When necessary, they have patience.** As essential as action is, it's also essential to prepare the ground that will lead to successful action. Preparation may mean helping people come around to accepting what needs to be done or waiting for the time to be right for taking the action that's necessary.

◆ **They are willing to take risks.** Since leadership is about meeting the challenge of change, a certain amount of risk is always involved. Good leaders minimize the downside of risk through discipline, preparation, and performance.

◆ **They display energy.** The appearance of vigor and the fact that you as a leader are excited and motivated and willing to commit yourself to spend time and energy to achieve what needs to be done can't be overestimated in terms of inspiring others. Energy in a leader infuses energy in followers.

Earning credibility is much more important than inheriting the right or the opportunity to lead.

Wise family business leaders who are family members recognize that their birthright gives them only limited credibility. They know that earning credibility is much more important than inheriting the right or the opportunity to lead. They prepare themselves through education and experience and by developing character. They know that if they play the "birthright" card with employees, saying, "My name is on the door, therefore you must do what I tell you to do," they will sabotage their credibility.

ONE LEADER'S STORY

When Amy Gutmann left her post as provost of Princeton University to become the president of the University of

Pennsylvania, the *Philadelphia Inquirer* ran an article on her approach to leadership. "My whole mode is to deliberate and then act," she said. But then she added, "It's a good thing in a leadership role not to be too patient. Otherwise you miss opportunities. To do good, you've got to *do*. To be a thinker is not enough."

Gutmann earned a reputation for being able to balance people's desires. "She's very skilled at listening, understanding everyone's point of view, and then bringing a group together. When there's a disagreement, she'll decide—but everyone feels heard," said a Princeton trustee. Her former boss said Gutmann "made decisions with judgment and respect for those affected." A former Princeton president said, "She has a furnace of energy."

While at Princeton, Gutmann oversaw the creation of a new science library designed by world-famous architect Frank Gehry. When Gehry said more money was needed for the project, she challenged him to keep within the budget. He did, and later he said, "I'm happy with it. The original design wasn't as strong as it is now."[6]

Do these comments about Amy Gutmann reflect a lot of what we have been saying in this chapter? Gutmann is an excellent example of an effective leader, and although she doesn't lead a family business, we bet she could.

TRUST IS THE KEY

There are so many things about leadership that are paradoxical: being able to combine patience and action; being able to build coalitions while at the same time being able to step out in front and say, "This is the way we need to go"; being both deliberative and decisive; and being able to hear diverse voices but also able to bring the people behind those voices together.

Trust is the key factor in making all these paradoxical forces work to move an organization in the desired direction, particularly in a family business. Effective leaders give trust to those they lead and seek to earn trust in return by being trustworthy. They

EXHIBIT 5   What Leadership Is...And What It Isn't

Leadership is not...	Leadership is...
Telling everyone what to do.	Gaining support for one's ideas.
A specific "type" of personality.	Flexible. It meets the needs of the situation.
Management.	Visionary.
Holding a title or position.	Good planning and thinking about the future.
Self-interested.	Other-oriented. It is concerned with the good of the system as a whole.
Saying, "Trust me."	Being trustworthy.
Talking *to* people.	Making sure everyone is heard.
Insisting on respect.	Giving respect to those led.

demonstrate respect for their followers. They view communication as a two-way process and set great store by listening well.

Effective leadership is somehow larger than the individual leader or team of leaders. It transcends personal interests and desires and focuses on the best interests of others and of the organization as a whole. It means being flexible and meeting the needs of the time and situation. It is characterized by phrases like "I think we ought to consider this," "That's a good idea," and "Maybe we should look at the situation from this perspective." **Effective leaders possess the ability to express their ideas and to gain support for those ideas without commanding others to adopt them.**

An effective leader is someone who can understand where the followers are and what they are capable of doing, who can understand the task to be done and the overall situation in which that task has to be done, and who then can adjust his or her style of leadership to meet those variables. When you are that kind of leader, you become not "the boss" but often the most flexible person in the organization, able to adjust to what's needed to serve it and move it forward.

Chapter 5

Where Leadership Comes From

Leaders can come from almost anywhere in a family business system. It is important to develop a sense for recognizing leadership when you see it and recognizing leaders who can provide it. When a business-owning family does that, it enhances its ability to nurture and select effective leaders. The point is not to pass up good leadership when it's right under your nose.

Opportunities for leadership can come from many different situations but frequently come from being in the right place at the right time. There's a lot of truth to the old saying, "Success is when preparedness meets opportunity." Another way of saying it is that leadership means recognizing opportunities and moving to take advantage of them.

PLEASANT SURPRISES

Sometimes, leadership comes from surprising places. In one family meeting, a third-generation family member stood up and urged his cousins to agree to a much-needed action. The cousins were stunned, because the decision he was proposing, while in the best interest of the whole family, would result in great financial sacrifice for this young man. No one else had dared to even mention such a proposal for fear he would erupt, and all were relieved when their cousin stepped forward and suggested it himself. Essentially, he broke a logjam and the family and its business were able to move forward.

In another case, Lydia, who was pursuing a career as a social worker, became seriously ill. Forced to quit her job, she came home to live with her mother and father while she convalesced. Her parents had opened a sports center, devoted primarily to soccer and basketball training for youngsters, and they hoped that their youngest son, Jeffrey, who worked in the company, would run it one day. Three other adult children worked at jobs outside the company and lived in other parts of the country.

As Lydia's health improved, she began to observe what was going on in the family business and in the industry itself, and she began to make some suggestions of her own. With her parents' blessing, she turned one room of the facility into a snack bar filled with video games and she ran the concession herself. It was a hit. Soon, she added a retail shop selling sports clothing and gear. It, too, was a success. Before long, her additions became more profitable than the other areas of the business. And she had still more ideas. "Let's add a rock-climbing wall and introduce in-line roller hockey," she said.

Her parents were beginning to have second thoughts about their son becoming the next CEO. Lydia clearly had more vision and superior leadership skills. She was also more creative and had a deep understanding of the needs of the customers. Her parents finally decided that Lydia would be the better choice for all concerned. With her greater ability, she would grow the company far beyond what had been originally imagined and her brother would be assured of a job and his family would be well supported. With the help of the other siblings in the family, Jeffrey was persuaded that Lydia was the right person to meet the leadership needs of the business.

Had Lydia not become ill, no one would have ever envisioned her as the leader of a thriving sports business. Yet, here she was.

"INVISIBLE" LEADERS

Frequently, people who aren't in an official leadership position provide some of the most able leadership. Often, leadership is happening and it's just not perceived as leadership because it doesn't fit the take-charge, tell-'em-what-to-do stereotype. It pays to look beyond the obvious.

In families and other organizations you often see people who are quiet and unassertive, but when crisis strikes, they're the rock that everybody leans on. If you ask who the leader of the family is, people probably wouldn't name that soft-spoken, unassuming individual. Nevertheless, when the time is appropriate, he or she steps up and is willing to lead.

Situations other than a crisis may also surface additional leaders. As we said earlier, not everyone can be CEO, but that doesn't mean that there isn't a potential leadership role of some sort for every family member who is willing to provide leadership. Some people excel at helping children understand what it means to be a member of a business-owning family. Others are very good at helping the family assemble and maintain its history. Still others plan family events or bring generational groups together.

Some individuals find that they can bring about more change when they are not in the most visible leadership positions. One may publish the family newsletter and, in so doing, may put issues on the table that are otherwise avoided. Another may raise issues at family meetings. When people do this, they are not only contributing leadership of their own but may also be a catalyst, stirring the "official" leader to sharpen his or her leadership skills.

FABULOUS "OUTSIDERS"

We have seen excellent family business leadership come from individuals who are not working in the business. One family hired a non-family CEO after the founding CEO, Richard, died unexpectedly. But the family wanted to maintain visible family leadership in some way and appointed Richard's daughter, Randi, to be chairman of the board. Randi had never worked in the company as an adult, but she had honed her leadership skills sitting on volunteer boards and presiding over numerous community events. Naming Randi chairman was the perfect move. Her experience imbued her with what seemed like a natural ability to lead the family business board without trying to micromanage the non-family CEO. Under the combination of leadership provided by Randi and the CEO, the business is thriving.

We are seeing women like Randi increasingly emerging as the chair of their family business's board of directors. They often have not been very active in the business. They may have been involved early on but then left to raise their children. Because of their families, they became involved in schools and other organizations related to their children and moved into leadership positions. As their children grew older, these women became involved in religious organizations or community activities, again rising to leadership positions. Through their participation in community organizations, they became educated in organizational structure and at the same time developed leadership skills.

During this time, they were also attending family meetings and becoming active in a family council, sometimes emerging as council chairperson. Through this kind of participation, they were becoming increasingly fluent in the language of business and in the particulars of their own family's business. They developed coalition-building skills within their family and within the ownership group. They were not seen as CEO material because they didn't have the appropriate experience in the business, nor had they risen through the ranks. But they did have the leadership skills and the understanding to fill the chairperson's slot, surrounded by carefully selected independent directors.

Rising to leadership as an "outsider" is not necessarily a gender-oriented occurrence. Men also do it. Family members outside the family business often gain tremendous leadership skills and experience that can be used for the benefit of the family and its business. They may head a school board, start a museum, or hold an executive position in someone else's company. The skills and the credibility they gain elsewhere can translate to leadership for a family business, so don't overlook them.

CONSIDER ALL THE POSSIBILITIES

Sometimes leadership comes from what the system might consider to be the least likely sources. As an example, have you ever stopped to consider how much leadership ability has been lost to family businesses because leadership positions were (and in much of the world, still are) limited to the male members of the family? When your leadership pool is cut in half, how can you be sure your business and your family are getting the best leaders available to it?

Sometimes families limit leadership to blood members, leaving out the in-laws. When they do that, are they losing a valuable source of leadership? It's a question worth asking.

EXHIBIT 6 **Look beyond the Obvious for Family Business Leaders**

— Family members who successfully pursue careers outside the business can make significant contributions to family leadership and to the board.

— Family members who gain leadership experience in volunteer work and community organizations might be extraordinary board leaders.

— Non-family executives can be major assets, serving as CEO or COO or playing other critical roles when family members are not able or available.

— Family members who are quiet and unassuming may have hidden leadership qualities. Who do family members seem to trust and respect most? Consider them for family council leadership roles.

— Motivated high school and college students can lead activities involving family members of their own generation.

Consider all the possibilities, understanding that leadership can come from anywhere, and so can the opportunities to lead. Look at how Randi seized the opportunities that she saw and how her family recognized a shining leader from an unexpected source. And remember that leadership bubbles up as well as filters down. You can provide leadership wherever you are, quietly introducing improvements to the department that you oversee in the business or serving actively on a family council committee.

Chapter 6

Never Underestimate the Power of Family Leadership

What is the secret to long-lasting success in a family business? Many family business owners will tell you that it's a healthy family—one in which family members care for one another, have fun together, put the good of the family above personal self-interest, see to the development of all individuals so that they can reach their full potential, communicate effectively with one another, and make decisions as a group about matters that concern them all.

That's a tall order for any family and **it takes leadership that's every bit as skillful and knowledgeable as the leadership of the business**. There's a tendency in family businesses to focus attention on the enterprise and on business leadership. But **business-owning families need to focus just as diligently on the family itself and on its leadership. For without a strong family behind it, the business will not survive into the future as a family enterprise.**

We introduced the notion of family leadership in Chapter 2. Let's look now at how it might work in the "Mercer" family, a composite of many business-owning families that we know:

Lowell Mercer, 31, and his cousin, Kendra Mercer Hughes, 35, were never interested in working for Mercer Stone, the business founded by their grandfather. Lowell chose to be a high school math teacher and is now aiming at becoming a school administrator. Kendra, an attorney with two elementary-school children, has her own family law practice.

Mercer Stone was once just a small retail outlet providing stone and marble for home construction, landscaping, and patios. Now it's a growing chain with 60 centers in eight states. Lowell and Kendra are proud of Mercer Stone and, early in their careers, they often talked with each other about how they could remain close to the company. Even though they were destined to be shareholders of the company one day, they worried that they might not be considered "real" family members—like the five cousins in their generation who were now working in the company. They guessed that other cousins not working in the business might feel the same way.

Then Kendra had a revelation. "I know!" she said. "We'll become like Aunt Janet." Aunt Janet, a homemaker with considerable volunteer experience, is married to Uncle Lou, one of the three second-generation brothers now running Mercer Stone. The other two brothers are Lowell's and Kendra's fathers. Lowell's dad, Martin, is the CEO.

All the Mercers think Aunt Janet is special. After Grandma Mercer, the founder's wife, died, the family flailed about for a while because it seemed like no one was there to hold it together like she did. Then Aunt Janet stepped in. First she started having the whole family to dinner at least once a month, the way Grandma Mercer used to do. Then she started organizing other fun events, like family picnics and other outings.

But more important, she took the family's pulse and acted on what she found. Martin wanted his son to join the business, but when Aunt Janet learned that young Lowell had his heart set on being a teacher, she helped Martin accept that decision. She quietly mediated disputes between family members. She suggested that a family employment policy be developed while the third-generation family members were still young. Family members see Aunt Janet as wise and strong, and they all feel comfortable with her. Most of all, they trust her because they know she has the interests of the family at heart.

What Kendra and Lowell came to realize was that the family needed an eventual replacement for Aunt Janet's leadership of the family, just as Aunt Janet had replaced the informal leadership that Grandma Mercer had provided. Now, however, with the business and family both growing larger and more complex, Kendra and Lowell knew that family leadership would need to become more formal. They organized a family council and persuaded Aunt Janet to be its first president. They invited one cousin to organize a family meeting. Another cousin initiated a family newsletter and hoped it would help those who lived far away feel more connected to the family. Still another thought a family retreat would be a good idea and won support for organizing it. Even family members in the business began to turn to the family leaders for assistance in specific areas. "We need a family values statement to help the whole company understand what we as a family stand for in this business," Martin said. "Can the family council assign a committee to develop one?"

And so it went. While the five cousins inside the business began to assume leadership positions there, their spouses and the cousins outside the business began to find ways to stay close to one another and support the business they loved by assuming equally important leadership roles in the family.

WHAT FAMILY LEADERS DO

The title of this chapter refers to the power of family leadership. And indeed, it can be very powerful in influencing the direction of the family, helping the family develop a framework of guidance for what it wants the business to be, and for helping the family define its expectations for the performance of the business.

But this chapter could just as easily have been called "Never Underestimate the *Value* of Family Leadership," because this kind of leadership is so critical to the family and, ultimately, to its enterprise. The principles of leadership described in Chapter 3 apply to family leaders as well as to business leaders. However, the *content* of family leadership differs markedly. Here is what family leadership does:

♦ Helps family members develop a perception of themselves as a *family*, not as just a group of shareholders. This becomes especially critical in the cousin generation, when family ties begin to loosen because more family members live far away and the family becomes more diverse.

♦ Builds family cohesiveness by nurturing relationships. This can mean seeing to it that there are ample opportunities for family members to have fun together. It can also mean bridging conflicts and differences between different groups in the family—for example, those who work in the business and those who don't, those who own shares and those who don't, or the older generation and the younger family members.

♦ Makes clear—through family values statements, family mission statements, and other documents—what the values of the family are. It also makes sure these values are adequately communicated so that they serve as guidelines to both the family and the business.

♦ Initiates the establishment of policies for the family, such as a code of conduct or a policy guiding family philanthropy. It also leads in the development of policies regarding the family's involvement in or relationship to the business, such as a family employment policy or a policy setting forth rules about how family members will communicate about the business to the outside world. (Please see *Developing Family Business Policies: Your Guide to the Future.*)

♦ Makes sure that all family members are heard (and not just those in the business or on the board). It invites the opinions of those who are not owners—such as spouses and others whose lives are affected by the business and the decisions of the family.

> Family leadership advances the family. When the family advances, it is more able to support the growth and advancement of the business.

◆ Assures that all in the family have equal standing as family members, whether they work in the business or not, and that all are treated as fairly as possible.

◆ Defines and redefines the family, constantly re-evaluating, reinterpreting, and updating "what our family is all about."

◆ Sees to it that family members learn how family businesses function. Family leadership also provides educational opportunities to help family members understand business fundamentals so they can be effective shareholders.

In essence, as we noted in Chapter 2, family leadership advances the *family*. And when the family advances, it is more able to support the growth and advancement of the business.

A VALUABLE ADVANTAGE

The need for family leadership gives family businesses an advantage that other businesses do not enjoy: the ability to provide leadership development experiences and opportunities to family members who are not employed in the business. Such involvement gives these family members a chance to shine and to be appreciated. In addition, it cements their connection to the family and their passion for the family legacy, its business.

As we suggested earlier, the challenging opportunities available include leading a family council; heading or serving on committees that address themselves to such tasks as developing family policies or planning family retreats or reunions; or overseeing the family's philanthropy. They could also include planning family participation in business milestones, such as a 50th anniversary celebration, or creating a documentary about the family business's history. Whatever leadership roles are chosen, they are serious jobs and they require talent and dedication.

Of particular significance, we find, is the opportunity family leadership roles provide to women in business-owning families. While more women than ever before are working in their families' companies, many are choosing careers outside the company, are delaying or interrupting careers while they raise families, or are forgoing careers altogether and making their contribution to society through volunteer work. The need for family leadership gives women not in the business an opportunity to gain leadership experience or to contribute to the family the valuable skills they've acquired in other careers or in community organizations. Increasingly, we are seeing such women emerge as chairpersons of their family business boards of directors. They may not have the experience necessary to be a CEO, but they have gained the knowledge, coalition-building skills, and other talents needed to serve effectively in overseeing a board.

In that chief emotional officers help to build and maintain family cohesiveness and strength, their role is crucial to long-term family and business success.

As we like to say, good family businesses have two CEOs. The chief executive officer leads the business and the chief emotional officer provides leadership for the family. In that chief emotional officers help to build and maintain family cohesiveness and strength, their role is crucial to long-term family and business success.

One last word about family leadership: Be conscious of the need for it and plan for it. Don't underestimate its importance

---

EXHIBIT 7 Eight Ways that Family Leaders Contribute

1. They strengthen the family's perception of itself as a family.
2. They build family unity by nurturing relationships and encouraging family fun.
3. They enable the family to clarify its values.
4. They initiate policies that guide the family and the business.
5. They make sure that all family members are heard.
6. They assure that all in the family have an equal standing as family members and that all are treated as fairly as possible.
7. They define and update "what our family is all about."
8. They provide opportunities for family members to learn about business and become effective shareholders.

---

to your family or your business, and don't hope that it will just happen by accident. It is just as critical as the leadership of your business and it needs just as much attention.

Chapter 7

Developing Tomorrow's Leaders

W hat can members of the senior generation do to help young leaders emerge? Plenty.

The ideas we offer here are what you might call big-picture ideas. That is, they focus on creating a climate in which the notion of leadership excellence can flourish. For the step-by-step particulars of preparing young people for future leadership roles, we refer you to other books published in this series, *Family Business Succession: The Final Test of Greatness* and *Nurturing the Talent to Nurture the Legacy: Career Development in the Family Business*.

CREATING THE CLIMATE

One of the most important things you can do is create an environment in which young people come to embrace the concept that being a leader is a desirable goal. That may sound silly. You may be saying, "Of course being a leader is a good thing!"

However, how many times have you heard people in leadership roles disparage their positions? Probably fairly often. "I don't know how they talked me into this," they lament. "I never have time for anything else." In some family business cultures, leadership is avoided, not aspired to—a burden that an unlucky family member gets stuck with. This view may reduce conflict among otherwise competitive siblings. But on the whole, such an atmosphere is undesirable.

To assure the emergence of future leaders, you must have young people who aspire to leadership. That requires a culture in which leadership is appreciated and honored. You go a long way toward building that kind of environment when you acknowledge and praise the qualities that make different people in your family effective leaders. "By running the company, Uncle Will is making a great contribution to our family and to our community," you might point out. Or, "Aunt Bernice is a leader, too, because she's the one who really makes our family reunions so much fun. She's great at pulling people together and delegating responsibility."

Create an environment in which young people come to embrace the concept that being a leader is a desirable goal.

You can help next-generation family members, from the time they are young children, understand what leadership is all about. You can help them see that being a leader will enable them to use their gifts and talents to contribute to the world around them and will also bring many rewards—perhaps wealth and prestige but, more important, the joy and satisfaction that come with helping others or building an enterprise.

It is important to instill in younger people the knowledge that leadership begins with the recognition of the opportunity to provide leadership. Make sure they understand that they need to keep their eyes open and take responsibility. While you can be helpful, the work of preparation is up to them.

It's also essential that once they identify the opportunities, they ask not "What do I want to accomplish for myself?" but "What do I want to accomplish for all?" By consistently sharing that message and observing young people's behavior and giving feedback, you can keep them focused on the principle that effective family business leadership aims to accomplish what is best for the family and the business.

PROVIDING DEVELOPMENT OPPORTUNITIES

Once you have created the proper climate, you can turn your attention to the development of leadership itself. The more that young people get the chance to try out some leadership skills, the more excited about leading they will become. As you work with them, emphasize the fact that there are many leadership roles to which they can aspire. They may not be the top overseer and, in fact, they may ultimately be happier in a different leadership position. Whatever they do as leaders, they can make an important contribution.

Here are some ways to involve younger family members in the practice of effective leadership:

♦ **Give them the opportunity to develop their skills by delegating small matters to lead.** You can begin as soon as they are young teenagers, or even earlier, and continue providing them with more difficult leadership challenges as they grow into adulthood. Put them in leadership situations where, if they fail, they can learn without being embarrassed and turned off. Their assignments should also help them discover their growth capabilities and that they can come to informed decisions about how much and in what areas they want to lead. During this process, you can act as Coach and Counselor as well as the Delegating leader.

In the family, a younger member might be asked to plan an event for the family reunion and to include other young family members on his or her committee. In the business, in addition to the usual manual chores given to the young, you might delegate a special assignment, such as organizing an ice cream social for a small group of employees or making a presentation on company products as they relate to kids.

◆ **Encourage young people to assume leadership positions at school and college and in community and religious organizations.** Youth organizations, sports, and other extracurricular activities offer superb opportunities for practicing and developing leadership. High school and college students can edit the campus newspaper, direct plays, lead a choir, or be captain of the debate team. One mother was upset when her 16-year-old son organized a rock band until she realized how many leadership skills were required: recruiting musicians, working creatively and productively with others, coming to consensus on what music to play and how to play it, promoting the band, getting jobs, and performing in front of an audience.

◆ **Provide special leadership learning opportunities within the business and the family.** Some business-owning families create "junior boards" or "shadow boards" where older teenagers are allowed to observe and to interact with shareholders and others who are making decisions about the business. Or they might be brought into the deliberations of the family council in ways such that they can learn and contribute even before they're expected to take over responsibility. At McIlhenny Co., the Avery Island, Louisiana, family business that created and continues to produce Tabasco sauce, the board of directors grooms young people through an associate director program. Family members who participate in the two- or three-year program sit in on discussions and tackle "homework" projects, such as a report to the board on the status of the company's pension plan.

"It helps connect them to what's going on here," says Tony Simmons, a family member and the company's executive vice president. "It gives us access to some of our younger, brighter family members. We think it works well both ways."[7]

◆ **Help them set goals for themselves and others.** They'll need to establish educational goals, career goals, and leadership goals. And if they're aiming to be leaders, they will need to learn how to set goals for the organizations they lead and for individual followers. Use your experience to show how goal setting is done and encourage them to practice setting goals for others in their school or community organizations.

+ **Look for leadership-education opportunities suited to their needs.** One program tailored especially for members of business families is the Next Generation Leadership Institute (NGLI) at Loyola University Chicago's Family Business Center. It is an 18-month program designed to prepare next-generation family members to lead their family business. Other programs are offered by the Center for Creative Leadership in Greensboro, North Carolina. See the resources section at the end of this book for contact information.

Another source of leadership training might be your industry or trade association. Many of their members are family businesses and these associations want to see those members succeed into future generations.

PRACTICE WHAT YOU PREACH

Without a doubt, the most important contribution you can make to the leadership development of your sons, daughters, nieces, and nephews and your grandchildren is to be an exemplary leader yourself. When young people see in you the qualities of effective leadership discussed in this book, that will do more to teach and inspire them than you can imagine. They will learn from you the need to adapt their leadership style to the situation. They will see by your example what true delegation is. They will begin to recognize opportunities for leadership and understand that it's up to them to seize those opportunities.

There is one more way you can contribute to their learning process—a way we have not yet mentioned. If you are the CEO, don't try to solve all the company's problems before the kids take over. Hank, one CEO we know, was eager to make the transition to the next generation, but some parts of the company had

EXHIBIT 8   Seven Ways to Prepare Young People for Leadership

1. Be an exemplary leader yourself.
2. Demonstrate honor and respect for family members who are leaders.
3. Provide young people with small opportunities to lead. Coach them and give feedback.
4. Encourage their involvement in leadership activities at school and in the community.
5. Put them on family council committees or "junior boards."
6. Encourage the attitude of "What do I want to accomplish for all?"
7. Help them learn to identify leadership opportunities.

recently begun losing money. "I've got to fix this before I leave," he said.

We reminded him that when he took over the company, it had huge problems—it was in red ink throughout, its systems were antiquated, and communication between departments was almost non-existent. Hank turned things around.

"Now, Hank," we told him, "you don't want to leave with all the problems solved. Wouldn't it be great if some of the people of the next generation were able to tackle this problem and solve it? That would establish them as leaders for the next generation."

You can do the next generation a favor by leaving them with a challenge. Hopefully, they'll deal with it successfully and that will give them a boost in credibility and provide them with a tremendous head start in instituting their own leadership.

Chapter 8

Preparing Yourself for Leadership

Whether or not you become a leader is up to you. Even people who have leadership "thrust upon" them must make a decision whether or not to accept the role.

Good leadership isn't a matter of your own preference. It's really an issue of creating a company that is able to be successful in a constantly changing environment.

But let's assume you are a young person who aspires to leadership in your family business. How do you prepare? Reading this book is certainly a good place to begin because it gives you an overall picture of what effective leadership in a family business is. To give you a somewhat different perspective, we will reframe what you have already read here and offer the following seven broad guidelines for younger-generation family members:

1. **Accept that your No. 1 leadership challenge will be to foster change in the business while preserving the best of the past.** Part of your preparation, then, means being ready to lead change.

Change is constant, and only businesses that can respond to and initiate it will continue to be successful.

Sometimes next-generation leaders go to one of two extremes. At one end, they believe they shouldn't change anything "because this is a wonderful legacy that our parents have given us." That, of course, is a prescription for failure. At the other extreme, a new leader may want to change everything—not because it needs to be changed but because he feels the need to "make his mark." "Now that I am in charge," he may say, "I have a right to do things my way just as Dad and Mom had a right to do things their way."

However, good leadership isn't a matter of your own preference. It's really an issue of creating a company that is able to be successful in a constantly changing environment. And while change is necessary and inevitable, it should not be initiated whimsically or arbitrarily. It requires thoughtful, strategic planning.

2. Understand that you may need a different or better education than what Mom or Dad needed to start the business. Your challenges as a leader will be different because the business will be larger and more complex and because it will be operating in a different environment. If your mother was the founder, she was probably the sole owner and most likely a hands-on manager. When you assume leadership, you will have other shareholders—your siblings—to consider. You will have more employees and more managers and less opportunity to be "hands-on." You will need to oversee the development of policies and systems that weren't necessary when the business was small. All of this calls for the kind of education required to transform the company into a more professional organization, one that can thrive in a rapidly changing world.

3. Recognize that building your credibility requires a leadership-development process, and that you have to take responsibility for your own development. Other people will help, to be sure. We have suggested in the preceding chapter that the senior generation make different kinds of leadership-development opportunities available to next-generation family members. Review those ideas and, for a step-by-step description of a leadership-development process, please refer to the book *Nurturing the Talent to Nurture the Legacy: Career Development in the Family Business.* Take advantage of the opportunities for development that come your way, get the education you need, and seek the experiences that will enhance your skills.

4. Set aside the parent-child relationship that you have relied on and let the current leader—probably Mom or Dad—serve as your mentor where possible. This means learning to separate your need for parental love from your need for a mentor's feedback. Suppose you mix the two, expecting praise and then being hurt and disappointed when Dad is focused on what needs to change rather than saying, "You did a good job." You wreak a little revenge and push Dad's button by telling Mom and other family members about his inability to voice praise to others. It's a shortcoming Dad is already aware of, so he becomes defensive and you think you gain an advantage. But what you've really done is put yourself in a position to be the child who needs praise and support from your parent, and that is not a good relationship to have with your mentor. It's impossible to ask your mentor to develop in you the skills that you need while at the same time saying, "You're my parent and you need to prove you love me."

5. Realize that the succeeding generation—your generation—has power, too. All too often, younger family members say, "Well, it's Dad's company and nothing is going to change unless Dad chooses to make it happen." But over and over, we have seen dads who say, "I've got to keep running this company until those kids show some initiative and some interest."

Peter Senge, a pioneer in the field of management innovation, says that people frequently accept such myths as: "Significant change only occurs when it is driven from the top." "There is no point in going forward unless the CEO is on board." "Nothing will happen without top management buy-in." He suggests that other statements, heard from both employees and senior executives, are nearer the truth: "Little significant change can occur if it is driven only from the top." "CEO proclamations and programs rolled out from corporate headquarters are a great way to foster cynicism and distract everyone from real efforts to change." Along with other experts in his field, Senge suggests that people "cling to the belief that only the top can drive change" because "this belief allows us all to continue to hold the top responsible for whether or not change happens."[8]

So, leadership is not just the senior generation's responsibility. As an aspiring leader in the succeeding generation, you may feel that you don't have the opportunity for leadership because the older generation is still there. Under those circumstances, there are opportunities, but they may take forms that are hard to recognize. They involve building your own skills and credibility, learning and beginning to articulate your company's culture and values, and working on building coalitions, cohesiveness, and consensus among family members (perhaps starting with your peers in your own generation). Such leadership is subtle and has to be exercised within certain bounds. It doesn't mean that you're the grand leader who can articulate strategy and change the organization as you wish, but it does demonstrate trustworthiness, motivation, willingness to work hard, and other attributes that will stand you in good stead as future leaders are chosen.

6. Practice the four different styles of leadership—Directing, Coaching, Counseling, and Delegating. (See Chapter 3.) You'll want to make yourself comfortable with each style so that you can move easily from one to another as appropriate for the situation. Being limited to one style will inhibit your ability to lead effectively.

7. Develop and maintain an appropriate attitude. As a young person, you'll find it helpful to strive for a constructive and mature orientation toward the circumstances in which you find yourself. **Leadership is not undermining your parent.** Sometimes you may be tempted to head up a revolution in your family's business, but generally, that's not a good idea. You will gain more credibility by doing the more subtle things outlined above and you will strengthen your ability to make change when you have the leadership role. Besides, revolution runs the risk of creating ill feelings among family members and distracts focus from where the business should be going.

An important part of having an appropriate attitude is to be oriented toward providing leadership for the system as a whole or for some part of the system, as opposed to seeing leadership opportunities as occasions to get something for yourself. It's this "other-oriented" response to opportunity that allows you to provide leadership.

Being the owner's son or daughter, having a title, having ownership in the business—none of these can guarantee that you are a leader. Ultimately, **the opportunity to lead must be earned, and to earn it, you must have credibility. To gain credibility, you must prepare yourself.** Some next-generation family members may think they're ready to run the family business at a

---

EXHIBIT 9   Eight Ways to Gain Credibility for Leadership

1. Acquire sufficient knowledge to do the job.
2. Carve out a path that will assure that you get the experience you need. Take responsibility for your own development.
3. Adopt a mature attitude, one that includes patience and that doesn't seek to undermine your parents.
4. Recognize opportunities to lead, even though they may seem small, and take the initiative.
5. Earn people's trust by being trustworthy.
6. Be "other-oriented." Through your actions, demonstrate over and over again that your concern is for the good of the system and not just yourself.
7. Actively seek to build cohesiveness and consensus among the members of your generation.
8. Keep your ego (and your temper) under control.

relatively young age. But generally, people are not ready for the top role until they are well seasoned, with considerable experience and knowledge. Typically, in our experience, they're at least approaching or already in their 40s before they're really ready to optimally step into the top leadership position (although occasionally people in their 30s or even 20s prove to be excellent leaders). Preparation usually takes many years and a lot of patience.

Chapter 9

Following the Leader Is Leadership, Too

It's often said that to be a leader, you have to have followers. In our view, being a follower is by no means a minor role. When you're a good follower, you are, at the same time, exhibiting leadership. Consider these two scenarios:

Scenario #1. *In a decision engineered largely by his father, Thom, 38, has just been appointed the CEO of his family's business. This is a disappointment to his two brothers, who had their own hopes of being named to the top post. The younger brother, Keith, swallows his disappointment and continues on as marketing chief. "Maybe Thom will screw up and I'll get the chance to run this company," he says to himself, chuckling. "Maybe I can even help him screw up."*

Thom's older brother, Milt, takes the decision hard. He complains bitterly about Thom's shortcomings to anyone who will listen—his wife, his children, his mother, other family shareholders, and board members. He threatens to leave the company. A newspaper reporter gets wind of the conflict and publishes an unflattering story. Non-family employees, fearing a company meltdown, start to search for other jobs. Thom finds himself in the uncomfortable position of having to reassure bankers, suppliers, and customers that the company is stable. Outwardly, Keith sympathizes with Thom, but he offers minimal help and, truth is, he enjoys seeing Thom sweat.

Meanwhile, Milt's wife has forbidden their children from having contact with Thom's children. The entire family is splitting apart at the seams, and Milt's children are getting the message that if your dad doesn't get to run the company, your loyalty to him requires regarding Uncle Thom and his family as enemies.

Scenario #2. *Juanita, 40, has just been named CEO of her family's business. Her siblings, younger sister Charlotte and older brother Avery, have also aspired to the top leadership role, but while they are disappointed, they refuse to let themselves be devastated by the turn of events. The process of selecting Juanita was a long and fair one, involving the objective observations of some respected outside directors.*

"The important thing is the success of the company," Avery tells Charlotte. "Juanita will be a good leader, but she'll need our input and support. We know how to implement strategy. And, we owe it to our family to show Juanita we have confidence in her and to help her get this company where it needs to go."

"I have another reason for wanting to support Juanita," replies Charlotte. "I want us to demonstrate to our children that we can be gracious about not being chosen as Dad's successor and that it's necessary for all of us to pull together for the good of the family and the good of the company. After all, they're going to own this business someday. It's important for them to see that we can continue to work together."

Someone has to lead, or you can't really have an organization. And "followership" is important because an organization depends upon clear lines of authority. As we pointed out earlier, members of a sibling team have to adopt a different view of leadership than they likely grew up with. In most cases, only one of the siblings will have the responsibility of being CEO, but they all have the responsibility of being good owners, which means accepting their sibling's leadership and presenting a united front to the world outside the family. As a sibling (or a cousin), you ought to be able to say, "Okay, we differ on these things. My opinion may be in the minority, but what's best for all of us is for the company to be successful, and so I'm not going to do anything that will undermine the success of the company. I may state my beliefs at a board meeting or at a family meeting, but I'm not going to take that argument outside." That's good followership and it is a form of leadership itself because it sets an example for others. It is, in effect, leading by doing.

ACCEPTING LEADERSHIP FROM OTHERS

It helps to think of leadership as a *dynamic* in organizations, not as a person. Even though one sibling is CEO, the siblings can exert leadership as a team. Often what's best is that the group comes together and says, "We believe this is the direction we should be going." Or, sometimes when "the" leader, the CEO, is trying to gain acceptance for an idea, a group, such as the family council or the other siblings or cousins on the management team, can come forward and endorse the CEO's idea. That's good followership and, again, good leadership, and it has more impact than if the CEO is promoting the idea alone.

In the context of thinking of leadership as dynamic, it also helps to think of it as fluid. As the situation changes, a different individual or group may step forward and lead. One sibling on the executive team may be particularly good speaking for the family or the business in a crisis; another may have more talent in pushing a company forward when the waters are quiet. Without sacrificing his or her own authority, a wise CEO lets others lead as the situation demands and becomes, for a time, a follower.

Leadership in the family will also be fluid, and sometimes the head of the family council will step back and be a follower temporarily when some other family member has greater skills to lead in a particular situation.

PREPARING THE FAMILY TO ACCEPT
A NEW LEADER

The incumbent leaders can—and should—pave the way for the acceptance of a new leader in the next generation. Founders can do much to prepare the siblings to accept a brother or sister as the family business CEO. In turn, the sibling generation prepares the next generation to accept a cousin as the company's top leader.

The key is for the incumbent leaders to set in motion a successor selection process that does several things:

- Makes clear that the next CEO is going to be chosen to meet the needs of the company, not because of birth order or parental favoritism.
- Creates a climate for change, one in which the current leaders instill the idea that "there's going to be change in both our external and internal environments and we need to be able to respond to that."
- Enables all who are being considered for top leadership to understand their own abilities and be able to make a more objective assessment of whether or not they are the best choice for the CEO role.
- Is open and transparent, so that at least the family understands who is being considered and what the criteria are.
- Allows ample time for leadership development, self-assessment, and a final choice to occur. Succession usually takes 5 to 15 years or so. (For more information please see *Family Business Succession: The Final Test of Greatness.*)

We have often seen that, by the time the succession process is over, there really is some consensus among the siblings or the cousins about who the next leader should be. And while some individuals who are not chosen might feel a personal sense of loss at not achieving a goal that they had had perhaps since they were children, they nevertheless accept the choice as the right one for the organization and for the family.

When a family business reaches the cousin generation, it may not be able to absorb all of the younger generation members who want to work in the business. Not only do the incumbent leaders have to decide who the successor CEO is, but they may also have to make some tough decisions about who can and who cannot join the family firm. If they haven't already done so, business-owning families transitioning from their second to third generations should clearly establish family employment policies and encourage offspring to follow their passions into satisfying careers.

Having a good selection process in place and having outlets other than the CEO position for other able individuals helps to preserve family and ownership unity and to retain good talent in the business.

MITIGATING SIBLING RIVALRY

In the first scenario above, you saw that Milt and Keith let their sibling rivalry get the best of them and sabotage Thom's leadership. In the second, you saw Avery and Charlotte put in check any feelings of disappointment and rivalry they might have felt over the selection of their sister, Juanita, as the new CEO. They were determined to act in the best interests of the business and of the family. They understood that Juanita was chosen because she had the talent and ability best suited to the needs of the organization. They were also mature enough to separate their own need for achievement from the best outcome for the family's business.

They were able to sort things out according to the three circles we discussed in Chapter 2. From a management perspective, Avery and Charlotte each aspired to be CEO. But when they put on their ownership hats, they could say, "What I want is for this company to be as successful as possible and to grow the overall wealth that I participate in." From a family perspective, however, their attitude was, "I want my siblings to be successful too, and I want us to be able to pass this valuable asset, our business, to our children." By looking at the situation from three viewpoints, they saw the importance of separating their own career goals from their goals as owners and family members and focused on the success of the company, not their own personal success. As a result, they were better prepared to accept the decision that their sister was better qualified than they were to be CEO.

Ideally, parents will raise children in ways that don't promote sibling rivalry. They will make it clear that the young people's destiny is in their own hands. They will institute a transparent process of leadership development and selection. They will constantly make the point that there are many ways to contribute and many ways to provide leadership. Many business-owning families make a big point of saying, "CEO is just another job." And they make sure that the CEO position and its responsibilities and accountabilities are clearly defined, just as they would do for other jobs.

What if sibling (or cousin) rivalry still persists and is a danger to the family and business? Someone like Milt in your family may be saying, "You chose my brother to be leader and that proves you love him more than you love me." When that happens, it's probably wise to get professional family counseling.

THE ROLE OF TRUST

Essentially, good followership is the result of trust. When people see that the process of selecting a leader is open, based on objective criteria, and designed to yield what's best for everyone collectively, they can more readily accept the leadership of the one selected for a given position. When they see that the chosen leader is capable, listens well, delegates generously and wisely, and acts in the best interests of all, they develop trust for the leader and more willingly lend their support.

Good followership is the result of trust.

EXHIBIT 10   Am I a Good Follower?

1. Do I understand that when I am a good follower, I am setting an important example for younger family members?
2. Do I readily contribute my ideas?
3. When my view is in the minority, am I able to present a show of unity with my leader and team to the outside world?
4. Do I buckle down and do the job I'm asked to do? When necessary, do I go the extra mile?
5. Do I step forward and provide leadership when there is an opportunity and I have the appropriate skills?
6. Do I actively and openly support the leader so that others will do so, too?

Chapter 10

Overcoming Impediments to Leadership

The deck is stacked *for* leadership in an organization. The organization may not favor any specific person for leadership, but people in organizations seek leaders. So, the opportunity to lead is there, the role of leader exists, and somebody needs to play it. If nobody plays it, you have a severely weakened organization.

Given that organizations want leaders, what stands in the way of leadership? In a family business, impediments to leadership take many forms and frequently are self-inflicted. Here are some of the most common, with suggestions for overcoming them:

Impediment: The previous generation. "Dad just won't retire and get out of the way." How many times have we heard this from a son or daughter? An aspiring successor in the younger generation yearns for the time when he or she can demonstrate leadership but frets that Mom or Dad just won't let go of control.

Remedy: If you are the aspiring successor, exhibit patience, attend to your preparation for leadership (see Chapter 8), and build your credibility. Look for opportunities to make small and then larger and larger contributions to the system as a whole. As you do, the senior generation will gain more and more confidence in your ability to lead and may finally loosen their grip. It also helps to understand their perspective so that you can take action that will help allay their fears about letting go. Are they worried

EXHIBIT 11   Helping My CEO Parent to Let Go

Overeager Beaver	Patient Preparer
I've got to get Dad out of here. I need to make my own decisions.	Maybe I should take a look at myself and see if there's something about me that's holding up Dad's retirement decision.
Why won't he just let go? It's my turn now.	I'll make sure Dad knows I understand how painful it is for him to leave this business.
If Dad would only tell me what he wants, I'd do it. But I'll want him out of here before I act.	My siblings and I need to figure out what to do on our own and show Dad what we can do.
Doesn't Dad see that I'm the one who should succeed him? Why is he stalling about announcing me as the next CEO?	I'd love to run this business but my sister would also be a great CEO. I need to be sure Dad knows I'll support her, if she's the successor.
As soon as I'm in charge, my brother is out of here. What a loser! I don't know why Dad's been protecting him for so long.	We have to help our brother see that he's not right for this business. But we'll do it with love and help him explore other options.
What can I do to make Dad retire?	It's up to us to be prepared to take charge and show Dad we can work together.

about being financially secure in retirement? Are they afraid you and your siblings won't get along if they leave the business? Do they believe you're just not ready? (Of course, once young people finally get the opportunity to exercise leadership, they often find out that it wasn't just their father that was the impediment to leadership. They themselves were the problem—and now they can't blame the old man anymore.)

Impediment: Inability to let go. If you're an incumbent CEO who is hanging on despite closing in on retirement age, you may be an impediment to the leadership that your business now needs. In want of fresh leadership, your business may be stagnating. Your inability to share leadership with others can inhibit development of members of the next generation as tomorrow's leaders.

Remedy: It's probably a wise idea to take a hard look at what keeps you from planning your retirement and the transition of business leadership to the next generation. A good place to start is to read *Letting Go: Preparing Yourself to Relinquish Control of the Family Business.*

Impediment: Inadequate preparation. This can mean a lack of the right education or a lack of sufficient experience—or both.

Remedy: Think carefully about what experience you need and then systematically take responsibility for going out and getting what is required. Acquire more education if necessary.

Impediment: Inability to see and take advantage of opportunities. Much of leadership derives from "being in the right place at the right time," so having the ability to recognize and capitalize on opportunities is a critical leadership skill. Remember how in Chapter 4 we talked about the non-family executive who discovered the mess his family-owned company was in shortly after he was hired? That's what we mean. He saw the situation not as a crisis but as an opportunity for leadership and, as a result, he turned the company around.

Remedy: Don't wait for someone to "give" you an opportunity. Learn to see and actuate the opportunities that are there. You may need assistance in developing this skill. Mentors, books on leadership, and leadership courses can help. You will find some suggested resources at the end of this book.

Impediment: Being too impressed with your own birthright. In the United States, we look negatively on people who invoke their last name or their ownership in order to get employees to do what such bosses want them to do. While employees may grudgingly do what they're asked under such circumstances in a family business, they won't be seeing the boss as a leader and they won't be inspired to follow. They're not going to work at their optimum level and it's likely that the company turnover rate will be high. When you're part of the business-owning family, a similar potential impediment to leadership is being perceived as someone who is privileged.

Remedy: Obviously, it's important to avoid leaning on your family connection or ownership as a means of getting what you want out of employees. Instead, earn respect, trust, and credibility through adequate preparation and by developing the character and characteristics that are seen as appropriate to a leader. It helps to dispel a perception of privilege when you show that you are not afraid of hard work and when you demonstrate that you respect and value your employees.

Impediment: Rivals and rivalry for the leadership role in the family or the business. On the whole, competition is a good thing, but often it can mean that people have different visions about how things ought to be and so they pull in different directions. When people in an organization are focused on competing for leadership, they are not focused on leading the organization where it needs to go. Or, if an incumbent leader is challenged by a rival, the leader becomes distracted from leadership in his attempt to defend his role.

Remedy: Building a culture that values good process and a team approach and that also creates many opportunities for leadership will go a long way to rein in destructive competition in a family business. Good process includes having a talented board with independent members, having a family council to make sure the family is heard, and listening to shareholders and understanding what their goals and values are and what they want done. It also means establishing a visible, transparent system of accountability, which becomes essential in the second and third generations and beyond. Many a threatened leader has overcome competition by building coalitions and creating room in the leadership sphere for those who aspire to more responsible roles.

Good process includes having a talented board with independent members, having a family council to make sure the family is heard, and listening to shareholders and understanding what their goals and values are and what they want done.

Impediment: Inability to institutionalize leadership. In the founder's generation, leadership tends to be ad hoc. People look to the entrepreneur and say, "What does the boss say now?" And what he or she says constitutes leadership in the first generation of a business. But that kind of leadership won't work for subsequent generations, when the family and the business are larger and more complex.

Remedy: The family should anticipate that the business will need to professionalize its management and to plan for that. This means developing people, policies, systems, processes, and infrastructure. This, too, is leadership.

Impediment: Unwillingness or inability to change the way you lead. As you learned earlier in this book, there are four styles of leadership: Directing, Coaching, Counseling, and Delegating. Some leaders get stuck in one style of leadership and say, "That's what I am." As a result, they limit their ability to meet the needs of situations that require a different approach to leadership. Or, if you are an incumbent CEO, you may choose someone to be the next leader because you think they exhibit a particular style (often yours). Again, that may limit an organization to one style of leadership when flexibility is desperately needed. Or, you may choose someone with a style that worked for you when a different style is needed in the next generation.

Remedy: We have said this already but we can't emphasize it enough: **develop the ability to shift from one style of leadership to another as the situation requires.** And, if you are a founder and use a Directing style of leadership that is so typical of founders, recognize two things: (1) the style that has worked so successfully for you is not one that will work so effectively for subsequent generations; and (2) as you are preparing the next generation to be leaders, it becomes critically important to be able to move toward the Delegating leadership style.

If your children adopt your Directing leadership style, that may be disastrous for the family business. If, however, you thoughtfully and deliberately change your own style and if you communicate to them that you embrace the idea that their approach to leadership must be different from yours, you will be giving them permission to use the style that is most appropriate to the situation. And, you will be freeing them of the tyrannical notion that they have to lead just like you did.

Impediment: A physical impairment. Physical problems and outright disabilities can certainly obstruct one's ability to lead. But not necessarily. For some, such difficulties are but another challenge to overcome—a son with lupus takes over a company's leadership after his father dies; a business founder grows her company despite suffering from narcolepsy; and so on. Think of the late Christopher Reeve leading the cause for spinal cord research from a wheelchair after his riding accident.

Remedy: Some remarkable leaders find ways to counterbalance physical impairments. One family business leader we know has such a terrible stutter that he can't deliver speeches or even make simple introductions. But he's an incredibly effective leader because he focuses on others. He's able to project genuine interest in other people and concern for their welfare. Because they know he has their best interests at heart, his employees are willing to give the time it takes for him to communicate with them. They understand his meaning, even if he has a hard time saying it.

Many successful leaders who have physical impairments or anomalies acknowledge them openly. One who comes to mind is former secretary of labor Robert Reich. He is abnormally short, and when he arrives to give a speech, many of his audiences are startled and uneasy. He breaks the ice immediately, drawing laughter with a joke about his lack of height, saying something like, "I'm a little short today." Within a few minutes, his audiences forget his size and become spellbound by his rich, deep voice and his intellect.

Understanding the needs of the family and the business really defines what's required of leadership, so an impediment to leadership can be anything that gets in the way of or doesn't match up with meeting those needs. An impediment can be almost anything—a lack of vision, an annoying personality trait, or perhaps arrogance. Frequently, one's biggest impediment is oneself.

Prevailing over an obstruction to leadership begins with an honest determination of what the hindrance is. Whether it is within oneself or elsewhere, persistence—perhaps over a long period of time—will be the critical factor in surmounting it.

Chapter 11

Summary

A family business demands some extra dimensions from its leadership because the nature of family firms is different from that of other businesses. Family companies consist of three overlapping systems: the business, the ownership, and the family. The leaders of each system must not only have the talent and skills to lead their own entity but also need to possess some knowledge of and sensitivity toward each of the other systems. And, because family members are so committed to and involved in the business, there are more emotional factors for leadership to deal with.

Leadership in a family business must change to meet the needs of the business in each new generation. Not only will the leaders change, but so should leadership itself. The founder in the first generation typically runs the business in a very hands-on, authoritarian manner. What he says goes. He may have to answer to no one. But when his children take over, they need to work together as a sibling team. They must be able to function as co-owners and be willing to accept leadership from one another—or perhaps, from just one sibling. They will also need to be accountable to one another, and they will find it necessary to meet the challenges of a business environment unlike the one that faced the founder. To accomplish this, they will have to lead differently than their parent did. The founder's one-dimensional, authoritarian style will no longer be sufficient. Wise founders understand this, and help prepare their sons and daughters for a different kind of leadership.

Leadership in a family business must change
to meet the needs of the business in each new
generation.

So it is with the succeeding generation, when cousins take over. Again, leadership must change to meet the challenges and conditions of a new business environment. It must focus on the needs of even more shareholders. It must see to it that the business becomes more professional. And, it must establish a vision for the future.

There are basically four different styles of leadership: Directing, Coaching, Counseling, and Delegating. Each is appropriate at one time or another within any given generation, and aspiring leaders will benefit from practicing each one until they are comfortable with it and can shift with ease from style to style. Typically, founders use the Directing style, but they will serve themselves, their business, and the next generation well by moving into the other styles, especially Delegating, and giving their children a chance to see different models of leadership.

One reason the ability to move from style to style is so important is that leadership is situational. That is, each opportunity for leadership requires a different response from the leader because the circumstances are different. For example, a Directing style will be more effective when the employees are inexperienced or the business is in a crisis, but a Delegating approach works better when there's an experienced management team and the business has a sustainable competitive advantage.

Leadership implies the ability to move an organization forward, and that means that to be effective, a leader must be action-oriented. **Other attributes of effective leaders include vision, trustworthiness, a concern for the well-being of the system as** a whole, and the ability to listen to others and to articulate people's goals and desires.

Furthermore, effective leaders understand that titles and positions do not confer leadership. They may give an individual the opportunity to demonstrate leadership, but people are leaders only when they have followers.

The senior generation can be helpful in preparing younger family members for leadership by providing them with education and experience and delegating responsibility to them. However, the real responsibility for preparing for leadership rests with the aspiring leaders themselves. It is they who must learn to recognize and seize every opportunity to lead, seek the experiences and education that will enhance their capacity for leadership, and develop their own character so that others will trust and respect them and be willing to follow them. As their leadership abilities grow and mature, the senior generation can feel confident that they are leaving the family business in good hands.

Resources

Center for Creative Leadership, One Leadership Place, P.O. Box 26300, Greensboro, North Carolina 27438-6300; (336) 545-2810 or http://www.ccl.org.

Next Generation Leadership Institute, Loyola University Chicago Family Business Center, 820 N. Michigan Avenue, Suite 1416, Chicago, Illinois 60611; (312) 915-6490 or http://www.sba.luc.edu/centers/fbc.

The Drucker Foundation website: http://druckerfoundation.org/. Contains many articles on leadership by some of today's finest leaders.

Suggested Additional Readings

Developing Family Business Policies: Your Guide for the Future, by Craig E. Aronoff, Joseph H. Astrachan, and John L. Ward. Marietta, GA: Family Business Consulting Group/New York: Palgrave Macmillan, 2011. www.efamily business.com.

Family Business Succession: The Final Test of Greatness, by Craig E. Aronoff, Stephen L. McClure, and John L. Ward. Second Edition. Marietta, GA: Family Business Consulting Group/New York: Palgrave Macmillan, 2011. www.efamilybusiness.com.

The Leader of the Future, edited by Frances Hesselbein, Marshal Goldsmith, and Richard Beckhard. San Francisco: Jossey-Bass, 1996.

Letting Go: Preparing Yourself to Relinquish Control of the Family Business, by Craig E. Aronoff. Marietta, GA: Family Business Consulting Group/New York: Palgrave Macmillan, 2011. www.efamilybusiness.com.

Mary Parker Follett: Prophet of Management, edited by Pauline Graham, with an introduction by Peter F. Drucker. Boston: Harvard Business School Press, 1996.

Nurturing the Talent to Nurture the Legacy: Career Development in the Family Business, by Amy M. Schuman. Marietta, GA: Family Business Consulting Group/New York: Palgrave Macmillan, 2011. www.efamilybusiness .com.

Notes

1. Tagiuri, Renato, and John Davis. "Bivalent Attributes of the Family Firm." Working Paper, Harvard Business School, Cambridge, MA. Reprinted *Family Business Review*, Volume 9, Issue 2 (Summer 1996), pp. 199–208.
2. Aronoff, Craig E. *Letting Go: Preparing Yourself to Relinquish Control of the Family Business.* Marietta, GA: Family Business Consulting Group/New York: Palgrave Macmillan, 2011, p. 67.
3. Nelton, Sharon. "Leadership for the New Age." *Nation's Business* (May 1997), pp. 18–27.
4. Winans, Christopher. *Malcolm Forbes: The Man Who Had Everything.* New York: St. Martin's Press, 1990, p. 36.
5. Ibid., p. 49.
6. O'Neill, Jim. "A Quick Study." *Philadelphia Inquirer,* June 27, 2004, pp. M1+.
7. "McIlhenny Co., Makers of Tabasco Hot Sauce." *Family Business Advisor,* Volume 13, Issue 3 (March 2004), pp. 4+.
8. Senge, Peter, Art Kleiner, Charlotte Roberts, Richard Ross, George Roth, and Bryan Smith. *The Dance of Change: The Challenges of Sustaining Momentum in Learning Organizations.* New York: Currency Doubleday, 1999, pp. 10–14.

Index

The Authors

Craig E. Aronoff is Co-founder, Principal Consultant, and Chairman of the Board of the Family Business Consulting Group, Inc.; Founder of the Cox Family Enterprise Center; and current Professor Emeritus at Kennesaw State University. He invented and implemented the membership-based, professional-service-provider-sponsored Family Business Forum, which has served as a model of family business education for universities world-wide.

Otis W. Baskin is a Consultant of the Family Business Consulting Group, Inc., Professor of Management at the George L. Graziadio School of Business and Management at Pepperdine University, and the Founding Director of the Family Business Forum at the University of Memphis.

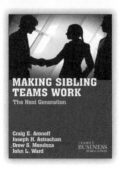

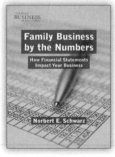